QUILTING
from every
ANGLE

NANCY PURVIS

16
GEOMETRIC DESIGNS

INTERWEAVE
interweave.com

ACKNOWLEDGMENTS

You know the old adage "It takes a village to raise a child." Nothing could be more applicable to this book. It has seriously taken a small village of women to help make this book possible. I now fully understand why quilting bees were formed. If not for my little beehive, I would have jumped aboard the crazy train. Thank you, Holly Reid, for piecing the Vertebrae Quilt; and Jenny Holt, Ginny Fisher, Val Weymouth, Liz Richardson, Nicole Skinner, Krystal Brown, Aleesha Bake, Sister Treu, Sister Judd, Linda Clark, and Ashley Morrissey for your special contributions. All of you helped in some capacity that allowed me to focus more time on piecing, quilting, and writing.

Thanks also go to my editors, Cynthia Bix, Jacqueline Maxman, and Kerry Bogert, for making this book a reality. Writing a book seemed like one of my wildest dreams, but you helped me show the world that if you work hard, it can pay off.

A special thank-you to all the companies who shared their resources to make this book happen, including Warwick Fabrics, Art Gallery Fabrics, In the Beginning Fabrics, Michael Miller Fabrics, Robert Kaufman Fabrics, Spoonflower, Moda, Aurifil, Gütermann, ODIF USA, Pellon, Pile O' Fabric Shop, Quilters Dream Batting, and the Warm Company.

My utmost thanks and gratitude go to my husband, Matt, for his constant support and devotion, especially in the most hectic of times during the creation of this book. Matt, with all the illustrations, basting, seam ripping, cutting, and pressing you did, you should get credit as coauthor!

DEDICATION

To my family—the best cheerleaders

CONTENTS

INTRODUCTION   04

INSPIRED QUILTING   06

PIECING & PRESSING TIPS   16

PROJECTS   20

Fossil Quilt   22
My Method: Making Half-Square Triangles   27

Colorblock Quilt   30

Brooklyn Quilt   36

Stones Quilt   44
My Method: Inserting Decorative Strips   49

Sequoia Quilt   50

Wayward Quilt   56

Split Decision Mini Quilt   62
My Method: Paper Piecing   67

Citrus Quilt   70

Mesa Quilt   76
My Method: Making Half-Rectangle Triangles   82

Kaleidoscope Mini Quilt   84
My Method: Sewing Y Seams   90

Circus Quilt   92

Desert Blooms Medallion Quilt   100
My Method: Making Flying Geese   110

Four Corners Quilt   112

Concordia Quilt   120

Vertebrae Quilt   128

Antlers Quilt   136

TEMPLATE PATTERNS   144

RESOURCES   158

INDEX   159

INTRODUCTION

After my mother passed away, my father gave me her sewing machine. It sat in my closet for many years until, when my son was born in 2010, I finally pulled out that old Necchi and taught myself how to use it. I started my blog, owensolivia.blogspot.com, to share my work.

In 2012, my blogging friend Danny Heyen (mommyfor-reals.blogspot.com) introduced me to modern quilting. It was something I had never heard of before. When I saw some of the great pieces she was making, I knew I wanted to give quilting a try. I began collecting fabrics

Setting bright half-square triangles in a pattern surrounded by negative space gives the Fossil Quilt (page 22) a distinctly modern look.

and became especially interested in modern graphic prints. I came to love modern quilting for its use of bold solid colors and prints, for its minimal look with lots of negative space, and for the geometric nature of many of its designs.

I'm especially attracted to the idea of using geometric shapes such as squares, rectangles, and triangles in new ways. I find it so interesting that simple lines, intersecting at various angles, can form such versatile geometries. Of course, these shapes and angles have been used in basic quilt blocks for many years. Yet people are still finding new ways to use them.

One of my favorite shapes is the half-square triangle (HST). Their simple diagonal lines make HSTs very versatile design elements. They are easy to work with, too, making them a great choice for stitchers of all skill levels.

Over the years, I have come to enjoy the creative processes of both designing and making quilts. I have discovered that what I really like most is the ability to see a design I have imagined come to fruition as a tangible, usable product that can bring joy and comfort to a person's life. If you have ever slept under a handsewn quilt, curled up under one with a good book, or tucked your child to sleep under one, you know the joy and comfort I'm describing.

I freely admit that I'm not a quilting expert; I just want to design and make quilts because I love to create, and I hope that is the case for you, too. I taught myself in a way that works best for me, and I hope that you can take these designs and work them in a way that best suits you.

This book features sixteen quilt patterns in easy to advanced skill levels, making it a perfect companion for a growing quilter. It also offers plenty for experienced quilters who want to expand their pattern library, because these designs can be reinterpreted in the maker's own way. I encourage you to let your style and personality shine through in your own versions of these quilts.

Sprinkled throughout the book in sections called "My Method," you'll find the basic techniques I used for making these projects. Because most of the quilts feature designs with angled shapes, I have focused on the methods I use to achieve sharp, accurate piecing: half-square and half-rectangle triangles, paper piecing, and Y seams. You may very likely have your own preferred methods or techniques, but here I share the ones that have worked for me.

I hope you will find inspiration in this book, and that these quilts will bring joy to you and to someone you love.

Angles can be dramatic, as in this mix of different high-contrast triangles in the Mesa Quilt (page 74).

Half-square triangles create drama when used in fresh new ways (Four Corners Quilt, page 110).

NOTE

Hashtags are a great way to connect to other quilters through social media. Under the quilt name at the beginning of each project in this book, look for its hashtag. Then, when you make and post photos of your projects online, hashtag them to share! You can also search these hashtags before you start your project for loads of design inspiration. Also, search for the general hashtag for this book, #quiltingfromeveryangle.

INSPIRED QUILTING

I encourage you to put your own individual style and personality into making the quilts presented here. For example, feel free to choose your own colors and mix up the placement of colors within the quilts. Perhaps making these quilts might even inspire you to create your own quilt designs. In this chapter, I share some of the process that led me to design the quilts in this book.

DEVELOPING AN EYE FOR DESIGN

If you want to expand your horizons—even just for making one quilt—learning to see things in a new light will help you achieve your goal. If you're interested in making a unique quilt that expresses who you are, cultivate your ability to spot interesting patterns and color combinations in your everyday life. Eventually, you'll find yourself becoming adept at using them to develop unique designs.

I gather visual inspiration from all sorts of places, and I can promise you that if you look up from this book right now, you more than likely have a few new design options staring you right in the face. The setting you're in—whether it's an art gallery, a park, or even an office—doesn't matter. Inspiration is all around you.

PATTERNS IN EVERYDAY LIFE

This earth and the people on it are amazing. The things that people produce through imaginative thought and problem solving blow my mind! Learning to recognize design in everyday life is not necessarily difficult, but it requires following a new train of thought when you're out and about. You have to teach yourself what to look for.

Here's an experiment: Go for a walk in a public place like a shopping center or a downtown street, and take along a small sketchbook, a pencil, and a camera. (I use my phone's camera.) Look for designs and patterns. Personally, I am attracted to things that people create, like buildings and other structures, because they feature interesting combinations of rectangles, squares, triangles, and other geometric and angled shapes.

I focus on things like architectural details, windows, railings, iron gates, flooring such as tile, window displays, and even graffiti. Look at everything, from bridges and electrical wires to cracks in the sidewalk. Notice more intangible things, such as shadows, or the intersection of two objects. And of course, study anything in nature, which, after all, displays living design.

Interesting colors, lines, and shadows, photographed by the author.

Sketch or take pictures of anything that inspires you. If you have to be that weird person in public taking awkward photos in awkward positions to capture the perfect picture, then go for it. (I have received my fair share of odd looks!)

Occasionally, you'll spot literal quilt blocks, like the floor tiles I photographed in London or the decorative wall tiling I shot in Provo, Utah (page 8). Designs that make use of geometric elements like lines, triangles, and squares are naturals for quilt blocks.

Color is a key component of design, so be sure to take note of colors you see. Keep an eye out for interesting color combinations in people's clothing and accessories. And look at colors around you in general. Colors and color palettes in nature are beautiful—naturally!

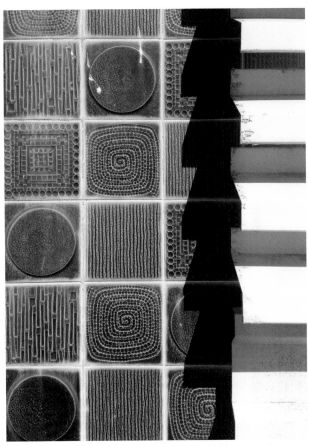

This photo by designer Heather Moore of Skinny LaMinx (skinnylaminx.com) shows great details of shadows and shapes.

TIP

When you take photos of people, do be courteous and get their permission first. I once approached a stranger and asked her if I could take a picture of her sweater because I liked the pattern on it. Really! Who does that? Well, I do. And in this case, she kindly obliged.

Tile floor in London, England, photographed by the author.

Tile wall of the Provo Towne Centre in Provo, Utah, photographed by the author.

EXPOSE YOURSELF TO DESIGN

Not only can you teach yourself to recognize patterns in your everyday surroundings, but you can also expose yourself to inspiring design. Go to museums and flea markets, or visit art and craft shows. Get inspired by those around you, and explore new avenues you may not have thought about before.

With the convenience of the Internet, you can find inspiration without ever leaving home. When my creativity is in a rut, I like to browse blogs, websites about design, virtual pin boards like Pinterest, social sites like Instagram, and online magazines. Take the time to browse new blogs that may not necessarily cover your preferred topics. (When you restrict your browsing to quilting resources only, you limit yourself to what you see other quilters doing.) Discover new artists, and read up on both established and up-and-coming designers in a variety of fields such as interior design, clothing, and architecture.

That said, I try not to browse the Internet too much—just enough to spark an idea that will send me to the drawing board to experiment.

I am not suggesting that when you find inspiration online or through any other means, you directly copy another designer's work. You can be inspired by what you see, but please respect the artist's work and ask the rightful owner

for permission to use his or her design if you plan to turn anything you see into a quilt design that you will display, sell, or publish. It's the law, and it's the right thing to do!

CREATE AN INSPIRATION BOARD

Once you start noticing designs and colors, you may start to feel a bit overwhelmed by all the new possibilities and ideas before you. To help manage and organize your inspirations, it's a great idea to create a pin board. This can be tangible (on a wall) or virtual. To see my virtual pin board that I share with everyone, take a look at www.pinterest.com/owensolivia.

On your computer, you will want to pin and keep anything that inspires you, including photos you see on the Internet and photos you take.

Using a real pin board is basically the same—a simple place to compile your visual interests. I mostly use a virtual pin board, but a wall display can look stunning and be quite useful. From bare walls to cork boards to metal sheets with magnets, you can create a custom pin board that fits your needs as well as personality. After my son outgrew his crib, I mounted the crib's metal frame on my wall and used clothespins to hang anything there that inspired me.

This photo by fabric designer Pat Bravo, founder and owner of Art Gallery Fabrics (www.liveartgallery-fabrics.com) shows her fabulous pin board.

TIP

When designing and planning a quilt, don't be afraid of these three things: your mistakes, your fabric, and other people's opinions.

Mistakes are inevitable, even for the best of quilters. Don't be afraid of mistakes. My best learning has come through mistakes, and it has made me a better designer and quiltmaker. Sometimes a mistake can lead to a new design, so embrace it.

Our beloved fabrics. Many people just can't bear cutting into their most precious fabric. If you're one of these people, save your favorite fabrics for designs you feel confident about. When trying out a new block design, I always reach into my scrap bin. After making the practice block, I will then use my good stuff. But please don't let your fabric sit for years untouched. If you're afraid to try something new, you are only limiting your design potential. Cut up that fabric and start sewing!

Trying new things can be scary. And what can be even harder is sharing your new designs with other people. People will either love them or dislike them, and if you're like me, you want people to love them. Don't be afraid of what others might think, though. By allowing others to judge your progress, you can set yourself up for failure or become paralyzed, which can ultimately affect your design potential. Your potential will only go as far as you take it, so try not to let others weigh you down.

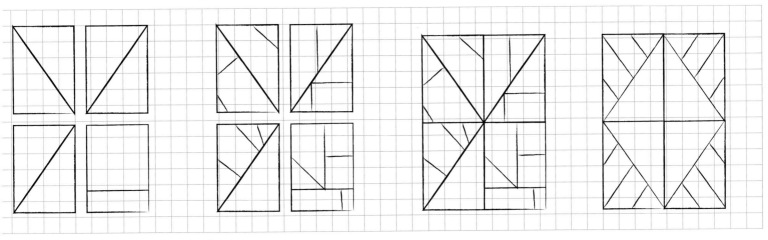

Sketches of ideas inspired by the photo

Resulting quilt block

EXPERIMENTING WITH QUILT DESIGNS

Once you have gathered inspiring images, review them and look for creative ways to use them. Can you tweak any detail you saw? Can you turn any of it into a quilt block? Sometimes you may try a literal visual translation, but other times you might just make one detail a small part of bigger picture. I think you will be surprised by what you find. Here's an example of how I turned a snapshot into a quilt block.

As you can see from this example, I like to experiment by sketching my designs. The majority of the designs in this book came from simply sketching. Sometimes the designs started out as simple shapes and lines that I kept tweaking until I had something I liked. If you're like I was when I first began sketching, you may feel that you don't know where to start. I recommend working with graph paper, because most quilts are designed around blocks. You can download free graph paper from the Internet (see Resources, page 158). Start filling in those little squares with simple geometric shapes—triangles, rectangles, squares, and octagons, to name a few. Play around with combinations of shapes and scale. You might be surprised at what you come up with. Use colored pencils to add hues in various combinations.

Left: Cracked concrete, photographed by the author.

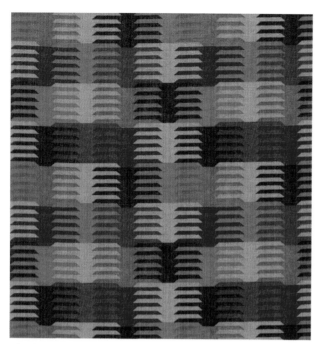

This beautiful fabric from Warwick Fabrics (warwick.co.uk) is called "Medina Watermelon." With the company's permission, I turned it into a pieced design for my Vertebrae Quilt.

Detail of Vertebrae Quilt (page 126)

Color card

COLOR TIPS & TRICKS

Choosing colors for a quilt can be a struggle for some people—including me! Here are some suggestions if you need a little guidance in making color choices.

→ Use a single fabric collection from a designer or manufacturer. A fabric collection includes a complete set of prints, and sometimes solids and/or near-solids, in coordinating colors that have been designed to work together cohesively.

→ Order a fabric manufacturer's color card. For example, the Robert Kaufman Kona Cotton Quilting Fabric Color Card offers a complete selection of swatches of the company's current solids (see Resources, page 158). If you wish, you can cut up the card and move the colors around to find a combination you like.

→ Check out popular websites like Pinterest that feature design inspiration.

→ Take note of fashion trends and what colors people are wearing.

→ Look at how interior designers combine colors in the rooms they decorate.

→ Turn to nature for color inspiration.

→ Study quilts made by your favorite quilters, and even check out artists' paintings, to find interesting color combinations.

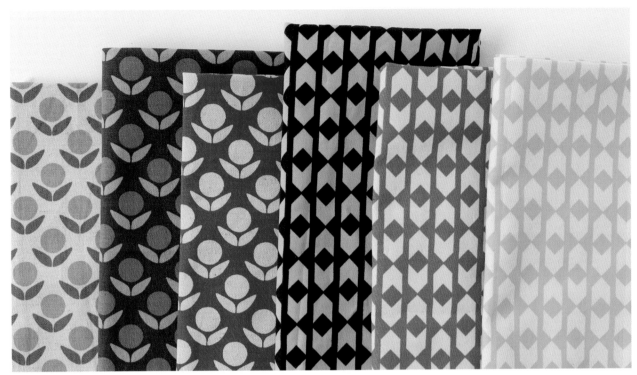

Fabric collection

Once you have selected some colors and fabrics you like, try the following strategies:

Walk away. So you picked out a color combination, but you're not 100 percent sure if you like it? Just walk away for a few hours and come back. You may see things differently with fresh eyes.

TIP

There are so many kinds of batting to choose from, including cotton, wool, polyester, bamboo, and various blends.
I generally use low-loft cotton batting because I live in the South where it is rarely cold, and so I prefer a relatively flat, lightweight quilt. For the projects in this book, I used batting from the Warm Company and Quilter's Dream Batting (see Resources, page 158).

I took this snapshot of a Dorothy Perkins fashion display at Scotland's Glasgow Airport in 2014.

The palette in this quilt block was inspired by the landscape photo below.

The greens, yellow, and blues in this scene would make a harmonious color palette in a quilt. Photographed by the author.

Take a black and white photo of the fabrics. This will enable you to see their values—their relative lightness and darkness—better than looking at them in color. When you work with a lot of different prints and colors, a nice balance and variety of light, medium, and dark values usually looks best.

Make a sample block using the fabrics you've chosen to see how they work together in your quilt's design.

Six fabrics in light, medium, and dark values.

The same six fabrics, photographed in black and white, show their values clearly.

FABRICS & THREADS

There is such an amazing array of fabrics to choose from! My favorites are 100 percent cotton and linen. My fabric stash includes high-quality designer fabrics, which I like because they wear well and are easy to work with. It's true that they can be expensive, but if you watch for sales and coupons, you can find good deals all the time at your local quilt shop or fabric store, or online.

All the projects in this book can be made using general-purpose threads. I personally like to use high-quality 100 percent cotton thread when I quilt. I mostly use Güter-mann for piecing and quilting. If I want my topstitching to show a little better or need a heavier thread, I love using Aurifil's 28-weight thread.

I find that I use white, off-white, gray, and black most frequently for piecing and quilting, because my quilting designs tend to be simple and not ornate. If you like variety in quilting and prefer color matching, colorful threads will be a good option for you, and many brands like Aurifil and Gütermann have a great selection of colors to choose from.

PIECING AND PRESSING TIPS

Here are a few simple techniques I use in piecing and pressing my quilt tops.

CHAIN PIECING

I do a lot of chain piecing for my projects. It's such a simple, efficient way to sew together multiple pairs of fabric pieces. It's also quick, and it reduces thread waste.

You put together pairs of pieces, right sides together and edges aligned, and feed them through your sewing machine one after another, not removing the sewn pieces or cutting the thread between pieces.

Stitch the first pair, backstitching at the beginning and end of sewing, and feed a new pair under the foot. Sometimes I gently pull the first pair from under the foot, and then feed

> **TIP**
>
> Place your paired pieces in order next to your machine to make it easy to grab the next pair. Be consistent in the way you stack and place your pairs. Having things cut and in order will reduce mistakes and save time.

Chain piecing

the new pair through. The units can connect to each other with threads as small as ⅛ to ½ inch (3 to 12.5 mm). When you are done, you will have a garland of fabrics. Clip the threads and press the seams open or to the side.

GLUE BASTING

As soon as I was introduced to glue basting, I was hooked—and I haven't looked back since. This method has saved me time and headaches when piecing fabrics. I used glue basting for all the projects in this book.

Glue basting simply means replacing sewing pins with washable glue to hold together pieces for sewing. You heat-set the glue with an iron to produce a temporary bond. I use glue basting when I'm piecing together blocks and long strips where seams need to match, or with tiny pieces that need stabilization. I even use it

when binding my quilts. (I don't use it to sew together simple units like squares, where the quick insert of a pin or two will do.)

Following are some important things to know about glue basting.

→ Use Elmer's Washable School Glue—the white kind. This glue dries clear. Do not use clear glue, which is runnier and makes a mess.

→ A little glue goes a long way! A great help in placing tiny amounts of glue on your seams are Fineline® Glue Applicator Tips from Pile O' Fabric (see Resources, page 158).

→ Glue basting works best on cotton fabrics. Always test a swatch first if you are unsure about the final effect.

→ Glue basting is not permanent. It will come out when the finished project is washed, or you can remove it with a damp cloth.

→ Until the glue is heat-set, you can reposition your fabrics if necessary. Even if it is set, you will still be able to gently pull the fabrics apart if you need to reposition.

→ Washable white school glue should not damage your fabrics, your sewing machine, or your iron. If it does get on your iron, clean it off with a damp cloth.

How to glue baste

1 When you're ready to sew a seam, place a few pin-dots of glue on the right side of one of the pieces of fabric to be sewn. I place it close to the scant ¼" (6 mm) seam line, but you can place it anywhere *in the seam you prefer. Generally, one dot at either end of the seam and one in the middle does the trick for small pieces. If you need more stabilization, you can use more dots or a thin line of glue. (There is no right or wrong, but*

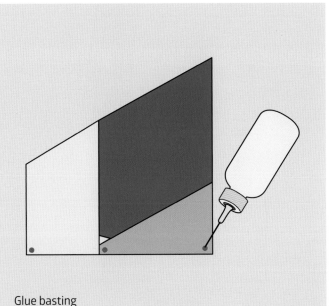

Glue basting

please do use only a little, because it will be a big mess otherwise!)

2 Place the other fabric piece right-side down on the glued piece, lining up any seam lines or points, if needed. Heat-set with a hot, dry iron for only a few seconds. Then sew your seam.

3 If pressing your seam open, gently pull open the seam, separating the fabrics. (Running the point of a small knitting needle along the seam will pop it open, too!) If you plan to press to the side, opening the seam is not necessary.

A PERFECT QUARTER-INCH SEAM

The geometric quilt designs in this book require accurate piecing to achieve their crisp, clean look. And for accurate piecing, your seam allowance needs to be consistent. Although ⅛" (6 mm) off may not seem like much, when you add ⅛" across multiple seams, it really does add up! Most sewing machines come with a ¼" (6 mm) foot and markings on the throat plate, but I find that performing a simple test of my seam allowance helps me achieve the most accuracy. If you do this simple test, you will know exactly where to sew on your particular machine.

How to test your seam allowance

1 Place a clear acrylic ruler under the needle and lower the presser foot. Manually lower the needle so that it gently touches the ¼" mark (**Fig. 1**).

2 Place four to six layers of washi or masking tape on your machine bed next to the ruler's edge (**Fig. 2**). This will become your ¼" seam guide.

3 Cut two fabric scraps 2½" × 4" (6.3 × 10 cm) with straight edges. Align one scrap on top of the other. Sew a ¼" seam, following the edge of the tape. Press the seam open. If the seam is accurate, the unit will measure 4½" × 4" (11.5 × 10 cm) (**Fig. 3**). If it does not, check your needle and tape and reposition them as necessary. Test again until you achieve an accurate ¼" seam.

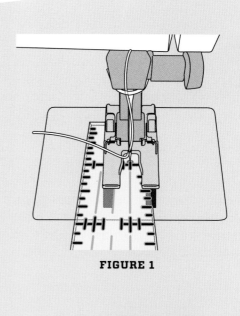

FIGURE 1

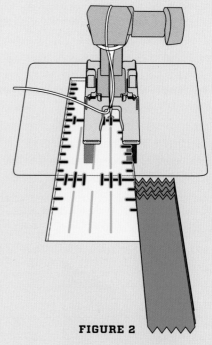

FIGURE 2

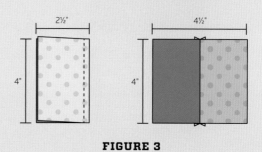

FIGURE 3

Over time, the tape will start to wear on the edges. I replace mine about every 5 to 6 quilts I make, but it just depends. Do not place tape over machine parts that need to be removed for cleaning, such as the throat plate. If your machine bed is removable, keep that in mind as well.

Note that even if you have an accurate mark or sewing foot, sometimes when you're sewing, your hands may ever so slightly move the fabric to the left or right, causing the seam to be off by just a few threads. If you wonder whether that's happening, place a ruler on the seam line after sewing a straight seam. If it is straight, it will run perfectly parallel to any of the marks on the ruler.

I find it also helpful to visualize the location of the fabric under the foot when it is fed through the machine at a perfect ¼".

PRESSING

I love to use spray starch on my fabrics. I buy a cheap brand at my local grocery store. For a few dollars a can, it does a great job of getting wrinkles out and also helps give the fabric a little shape before cutting or piecing. To avoid starch flakes, try this technique: lightly spray one side of the fabric, then quickly flip the fabric and iron the other side. Instead of starch, you can try a spray bottle of water. I use tap water, but I know some people prefer distilled water.

Some quilters prefer to press their seams to one side, and others, like me, prefer to press seams open. I am more experienced in lining up seams with them pressed open than I am with nesting, and it has become more of a habit than anything else. Sometimes the fabric wants to lie to a particular side, and if so, I will press to that side. (I like to call this "listening to my fabric.")

Press using whichever method you like best, but if you do press to the side, make sure to heat-set the seam first, then press along the seam line on the front side. This will help to avoid coming out with inaccurate units from the fold of excess fabric that can occur at the seam. And in general, always press toward the dark fabric.

My Favorite Tools

In addition to the tools and supplies that most quilters use, I have a few favorites.

→ I like three sizes of acrylic rulers: 6½" × 24½" (16.5 × 62 cm) (my favorite); 9½" × 9½" (24 × 24 cm); and 4½" × 4½" (14 × 14 cm). My most-used ruler has angles of various degrees printed on it.

→ For marking fabrics, I like to use a water-soluble fabric marking pen and sometimes a Clover Hera Marker to make creases instead of lines.

→ I use flat-head pins for machine sewing. Clover Wonder Clips, which are flat on the bottom side, are another wonderful option for machine sewing (see Resources, page 158).

→ For basting my quilt sandwich before quilting, I prefer Dritz Quilting Curved Basting Pins in sizes 2 and 3. To close safety pins with minimal movement of the pins and fabrics, I like to use a handy tool called the Kwik Klip (see Resources, page 158).

TIP

I like to keep a small craft iron plugged in next to my sewing machine. It helps me set the glue quickly without my having to get up or pick up a heavier iron.

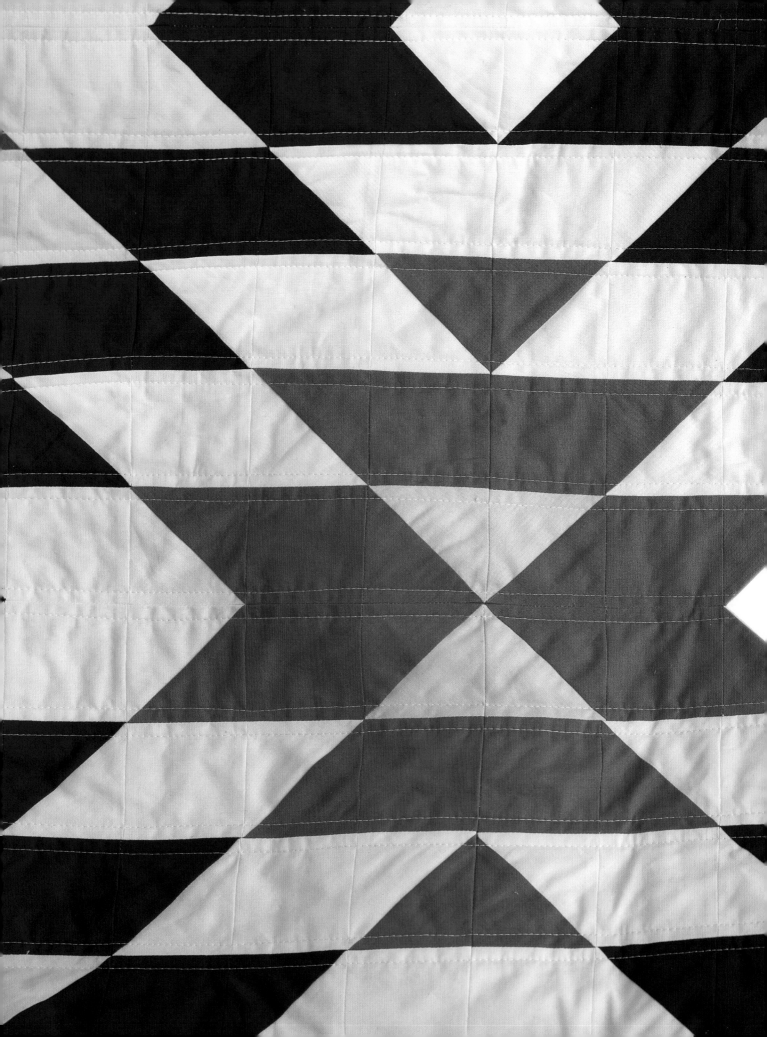

PROJECTS

In this section, you'll find sixteen quilts to make in sizes ranging from minis to lap size to a bit larger. Along with some of these projects are short illustrated tutorials for relevant techniques such as making half-square triangles and paper piecing. Feel free to skip over them if you already have your own favorite methods. For the four paper-pieced quilts, you will find the template patterns on pages 144-157.

Don't forget to share your results with your friends, using the #hashtags that appear with each project!

FOSSIL **quilt**

Fossil takes a look at lines partially unearthed—lines that, as with an archaeological discovery, cannot fully be explained until the entire image is before you. Its asymmetrical shape offers visual interest and makes you wonder, "Could there be more?" The simplicity of this design appeals to both genders, making it the perfect quilt for anyone. This size is equally appropriate for a baby quilt, a wall hanging, or a small lap quilt.

Finished Size
44" × 57¾" ¾"(112 × 146.5 cm)

Materials
Yardage is based on fabric with a usable width of 42" (106.5 cm).

⅜ yd (34.5 cm) red fabric

Scrap of red accent fabric

2⅛ yd (1.9 m) white fabric

3 yd (2.75 m) backing fabric

⅜ yd (34.5 cm) binding fabric

48" × 62" (122 × 157.5 cm) piece of batting

Cutting

WOF = width of fabric

From red fabric cut:
2 strips 5½" × WOF (14 cm × WOF); subcut into 14 squares 5½" × 5½" (14 × 14 cm).

From red accent fabric cut:
1 square 3½" × 3½" (9 × 9 cm).

From white fabric cut:
2 strips 5½" × WOF (14 cm × WOF); subcut into 14 squares 5½" × 5½" (14 × 14 cm)

2 strips 3¼" × WOF (8.5 cm × WOF); subcut into 22 squares 3¼" × 3¼" (8.5 × 8.5 cm)

1 piece 22½" × WOF (57 cm × WOF); subcut into 2 pieces 19¾" × 22½" (50 × 57 cm)

1 piece 23" × WOF (58.5 cm); subcut into 2 pieces 17" × 22½" (58.5 × 57 cm). From the remainder, cut 2 strips 11½" × 3¼" (29 × 8.5 cm); 1 strip 8¾" × 3¼" (22 × 8.5 cm); 1 square 3½" × 3½" (9 × 9 cm)

1 strip 3¼" × WOF (8.5 cm × WOF); subcut into 2 strips 19¾" × 3¼" (50 × 8.5 cm)

2 strips 3¼" × WOF (8.4 cm × WOF); subcut into 3 strips 17" × 3¼" (43 × 8.5 cm) and 4 strips 6" × 3¼" (15 × 8.5 cm).

From binding fabric, cut:
6 strips 2¼" × WOF (5.5 cm × WOF).

FOSSIL QUILT

MAKE THE BLOCKS

Unless otherwise indicated, all seam allowances are ¼"
(6 mm) and are pressed open.

1 Refer to **My Method: Making Half-Square Triangles** (page 27) and follow the Four units at a time
method using the fourteen red and fourteen white
squares 5½" × 5½" (14 × 14 cm). Trim the finished HSTs
to 3¼" × 3¼"
(8.5 × 8.5 cm) (**Fig. 1**). Set aside two of them for
another use. You should have a total of fifty-four
red/white HSTs.

2 Using the red accent square and the white square 3½"
× 3½" (9 × 9 cm), make a single HST. Place the squares
right sides together and mark a diagonal line from corner to corner. Sew on the line and trim ¼" (6 mm) from
the seam line (**Fig. 2**). Trim to 3¼" × 3¼" (8.5 × 8.5 cm).

ASSEMBLE THE QUILT TOP

1 Sew three white squares 3¼" × 3¼" (8.5 × 8.5 cm) into
a row **(Fig. 3)**. Set aside. Sew two sets of two squares
together and set aside. Sew eight squares together into
one long row and set aside.

2 To make the HST rows and columns, refer to the **Fossil
Assembly Diagram.** Before sewing, lay out all the
pieces according to the diagram to make sure everything is in the correct order. Sew together the following
units.

COLUMN A: five HSTs and the row of three white
squares from Step 2
COLUMN B: six HSTs and one set of two white squares
from Step 2
Row C: four HSTs, one white square, followed by three
HSTs
Row D: one HST, one white square, and one HST
Row E: six HSTs, one white square, and five HSTs
Row F: one HST, one white square, and one HST
Row G: six HSTs, one white square, four HSTs, and one
red accent HST
COLUMN H: six HSTs and one set of two white squares
from Step 2
Row I: one white square and one HST
Row J: one white square and four HSTs

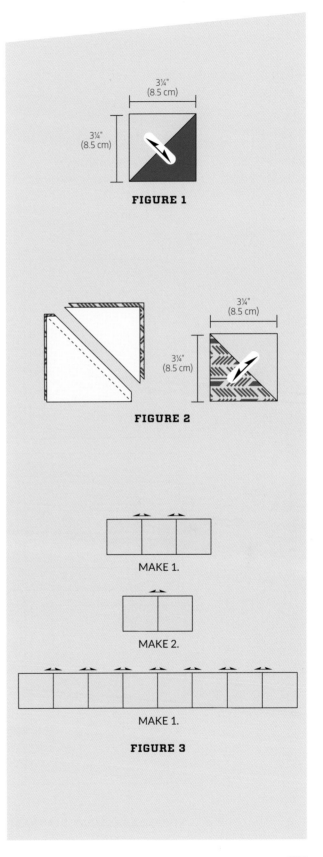

3¼"
(8.5 cm)

3¼"
(8.5 cm)

FIGURE 1

3¼"
(8.5 cm)

3¼"
(8.5 cm)

FIGURE 2

MAKE 1.

MAKE 2.

MAKE 1.

FIGURE 3

3 Refer to the *Fossil Assembly Diagram* to assemble the sections 1, 2, 3, and 4 for the quilt top.

4 Sew Section 3 to Section 4, sew Section 1 to Section 2, and sew Section ½ to ¾. Press.

FINISH THE QUILT

1 Cut the backing fabric in half to 54" × WOF (137 cm × WOF) and trim off the selvedges. Join the two long pieces along the 54" (137 cm) side. Sew a ½" (1.3 cm) seam and press open.

2 Use your favorite method to layer and baste your quilt top, batting, and backing. Quilt as desired. To fill in the negative background space and add textural interest, I did straight-line quilting in clean, simple parallel lines that echo the triangle theme.

3 Sew together the binding strips end to end, diagonally, and use your preferred method to bind the quilt.

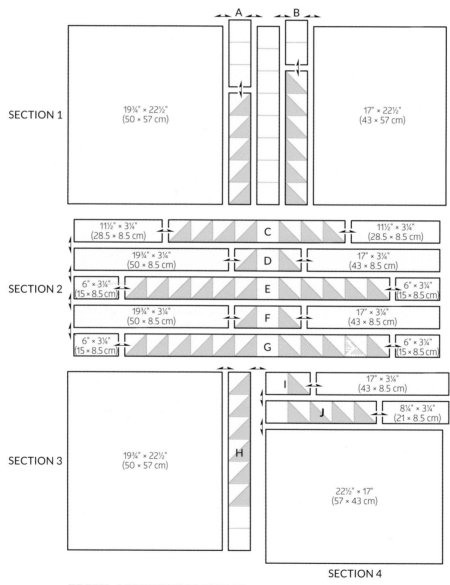

FOSSIL ASSEMBLY DIAGRAM

My Method: Making Half-Square Triangles

Many of the quilts in this book are made using half-square triangles (HSTs). It's amazing what an array of designs you can create with this simple shape. I offer two methods here—one for making four HST units at a time, and one for making two HST units at a time.

WHAT YOU'LL NEED

→ Washable fabric marking pen
→ Clear acrylic 5" (12.5 cm) ruler with a 45-degree angle mark
→ Rotary cutter and mat
→ Fabric starch (optional)

HERE'S HOW
Four units at a time

I really love this method because it allows me to make more units at one time. Also, I do not have to be as accurate with my cutting because the blocks are trimmed down in the end. Since this method results in bias-edged half-square triangles, I do recommend starching the fabric before it's cut to give it a little more body and shape.

1 Starch and cut out squares from two contrasting or coordinating fabrics as indicated in the pattern you are using.

2 Place a pair of squares right sides together with edges lined up and sew a ¼" (6 mm) seam all around the perimeter *(Fig. 1)*.

3 Using a ruler, mark two diagonal lines from corner to corner, creating an X. Cut along the lines. You now have four units *(Fig 2)*.

4 Open the units flat and press all the seams toward one side (preferably toward the darkest fabric).

5 Place one unit under the clear ruler, lining up the diagonal seam line with the 45-degree angle mark and making sure the unit extends a little on all four sides of the desired finished size *(Fig. 3)*. Trim the two sides.

FIGURE 1

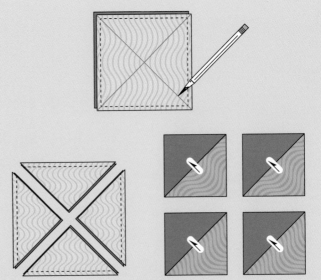

FIGURE 2

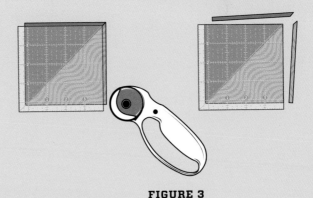

FIGURE 3

continued on next page

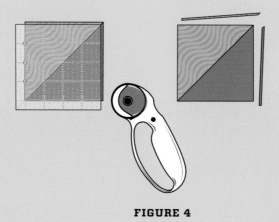

FIGURE 4

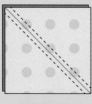

FIGURE 5

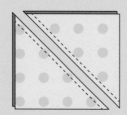
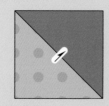
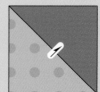

FIGURE 6

6 Rotate the block, lining up the freshly trimmed edges to the desired size on the ruler and making sure the angle lines up. Trim the remaining two sides *(Fig. 4)*.

7 Repeat steps 5 and 6 for the remaining units.

Two units at a time

This method is great when you only need one or two units. Even if I need just one, I like to hold on to the extra HST in case I make a mistake. The extra pieces can also be worked into the quilt back or into a future project.

1. Cut out squares from two contrasting or coordinating fabrics as indicated in the pattern you are using.

2. Place a pair of squares right sides together with edges lined up. Pin into place if necessary.

3. Using a ruler, mark a diagonal line from one corner to the other. Mark a scant ¼" (6 mm) line on either side of the diagonal line. Stitch along the lines *(Fig. 5)*.

4. Cut along the diagonal line *(Fig. 6)*. Open the units and press the seams to one side.

5. Trim the units using the 45-degree angle mark on your ruler, as in steps 5 and 6 for Four Units at a Time.

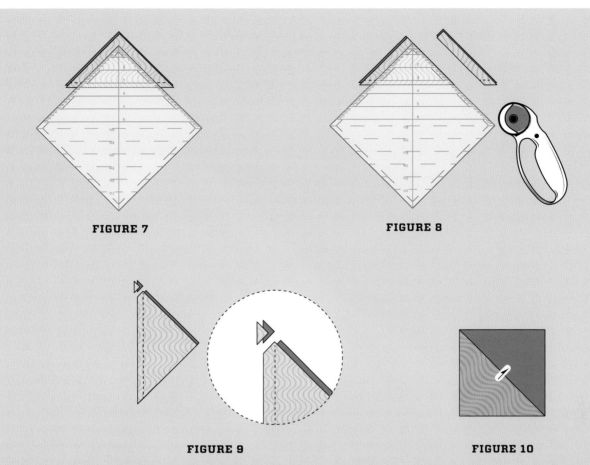

FIGURE 7

FIGURE 8

FIGURE 9

FIGURE 10

Option: Using a Special Ruler

Although my basic instructions call for a clear acrylic ruler with a 45-degree angle marking, I highly recommend purchasing the 6½" (16.5 cm) Triangle Square Up Ruler by Quilt in a Day (see Resources, page 158. When you are making lots of HSTs, using this ruler will save you time. It eliminates the need to trim the sides of a sewn unit using a 45-degree angle ruler. And instead of opening the HST and pressing before trimming down to the desired size, you do the trimming first.

1 Make HST units using either the four-at-a-time or the two-at-a-time method, but instead of opening them flat, leave them closed.

2 Line up the ruler along the stitched line of one unit *(Fig. 7)*. In this example, the desired unfinished unit is 3" (7.5 cm), so the seam is aligned along the 3" (7.5 cm) mark.

3 Trim the two sides *(Fig. 8)*.

4 Carefully trim into the seam, cutting off the dog ears *(Fig. 9)*.

5 Open the unit and press to the side.

That's it! You have a perfect unit that does not require lining up the diagonal with the 45-degree angle on an acrylic ruler *(Fig. 10)*.

COLORBLOCK
quilt

I love the traditional look of Log Cabin quilt blocks. Combined, they create a beautiful allover design with many variations. By focusing on just one Log Cabin block, I was inspired to enlarge this design. Making one side of the block with a single neutral fabric creates an interesting half-and-half design. I also created visual interest by replacing one strip with half-square triangles. This little quilt comes together really quickly, making it a great weekend project.

Finished size:
40½" × 40½" (103 × 103 cm)

Materials
Yardage is based on fabric with a usable width of 42" (106.5 cm).

¼ yd (23 cm) orange fabric

⅜ yd (34.5 cm) dark blue fabric

½ yd (45.5 cm) light blue fabric

¾ yd (68.5 cm) light gray fabric

1¾ yd (160 cm) backing fabric

1 piece 48" × 48" (122 × 122 cm) cotton batting

⅜" (34.5 cm) yd binding fabric

Cutting

WOF= width of fabric

From orange fabric, cut:
1 strip 2½" × 28½" (6.5 × 72.5 cm) (Piece 33)

1 square 2¼" × 2¼" (6.5 × 6.5 cm) (Piece 1)

1 strip 4" × 20" (10 × 51 cm); subcut into 5 squares 4" × 4" (10 × 10 cm) (for HSTs).

From light blue fabric, cut:
8 strips 2½" × WOF (6.5 × WOF).

Subcut as follows:

2 strips 2½" × 39" (6.5 × 99 cm) (Pieces 44 & 45)

1 strip 2½" × 33¾" (6.5 × 85.5 cm) (Piece 37), and 1 strip 2½" × 4" (6.5 × 10 cm) (Piece 4)

1 strip 2½" × 35½" (6.5 × 90 cm) (Piece 40), and 1 strip 2½" × 5¾" (6.5 × 14.5 cm) (Piece 5)

1 strip 2½" × 32" (6.5 × 81.5 cm) (Piece 6)

1 strip 2½" × 26¾" (6.5 × 68 cm) (Piece 29), and 1 strip 2½" × 12¾" (6.5 × 32 cm) (Piece 13)

1 strip 2½" × 25" (6.5 × 63.5 cm) (Piece 28), and 1 strip 2½" × 11" (6.5 × 28 cm) (Piece 12)

1 strip 2½" × 19¾" (6.5 × 50 cm) (Piece 21), and 1 strip 2½" × 18" (6.5 × 45.5 cm) (Piece 20).

From dark blue fabric, cut:
4 strips 2½" × WOF (6.5 × WOF).

Subcut as follows: 1 strip 2½" × 37¼" (6.5 × 94.5 cm) (Piece 41)

1 strip 2½" × 23¼" (6.5 × 59 cm) (Piece 25), and 1 strip 2½" × 16¼" (6.5 × 41.5 cm) (Piece 17)

1 strip 2½" × 21½" (6.5 × 54.5 cm) (Piece 24), and 1 strip 2½" × 14½" (6.5 × 37 cm) (Piece 16)

1 strip 2½" × 9¼" (6.5 × 23.5 cm) (Piece 9), and 1 strip 2½" × 7½" (6.5 × 19 cm) (Piece 8).

From light gray fabric, cut:
11 strips 2½" × WOF (6.5 cm × WOF);

Subcut as follows: 1 strip 2½" × 39" (6.5 × 99 cm) (Piece 43) and 1 square 2½" × 2½" (6.5 × 6.5 cm) (Piece 2)

1 strip 2½" × 37¼" (6.5 × 94.5 cm) (Piece 42) and 1 strip 2½" × 4" (6.5 × 10 cm) (Piece 3)

1 strip 2½" × 35½" (6.5 × 90 cm) (Piece 39) and 1 strip 2½" × 5¾" (6.5 × 14.5 cm) (Piece 6)

1 strip 2½" × 33 ¾" (6.5 × 85.5 cm) (Piece 38) and 1 strip 2½" × 7½" (6.5 × 19 cm) (Piece 7)

1 strip 2½" × 32" (6.5 × 81.5 cm) (Piece 35) and 1 strip 2½" × 9¼" (6.5 × 23.5 cm) (Piece 10)

1 strip 2½" × 30¼" (6.5 × 77 cm) (Piece 34) and 1 strip 2½" × 11" (6.5 × 28 cm) (Piece 11)

1 strip 2½" × 28½" (6.5 × 72.5 cm) (Piece 31) and 1 strip 2½" × 12¾" (6.5 × 32 cm) (Piece 14)

1 strip 2½" × 26¾" (6.5 × 68 cm) (Piece 30) and 1 strip 2½" × 14½" (6.5 × 37 cm) (Piece 15)

1 strip 2½" × 25" (6.5 × 63.5 cm) (Piece 27) and 1 strip 2½" × 16¼" (6.5 × 41.5 cm) (Piece 18)

1 strip 2½" × 23¼" (6.5 × 59 cm) (Piece 26) and 1 strip 2½" × 18" (6.5 × 45.5 cm) (Piece 19)

1 strip 2½" × 21½" (6.5 × 54.5 cm) (Piece 23) and 1 strip 2½" × 19¾" (6.5 × 50 cm) (Piece 22)

1 strip 4" × 20" (10 × 51 cm); subcut into 5 squares 4" × 4" (10 × 10 cm) (for HSTs).

From binding fabric, cut:
4 strips 2½" × WOF (6.5 cm × WOF).

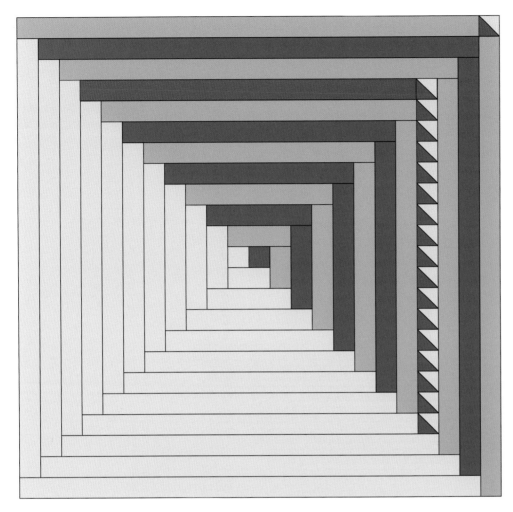

COLORBLOCK QUILT

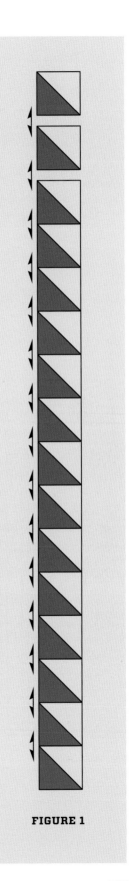

FIGURE 1

ASSEMBLE THE QUILT TOP

All seams are ¼" (6 mm) and are pressed open as they are
sewn. Lock or backstitch at the start and end of stitching.

1 Place the five gray and five orange squares 4" × 4" (10
× 10 cm) right sides together in pairs. Refer to *My
Method: Making Half-Square Triangles* (page 27),
and use the Four units at a time method to make a
total of twenty HSTs from the paired squares. Trim to
2½" × 2½" (6.5 × 6.5 cm). There will be two extra HSTs.

2 Sew together sixteen HSTs into a long vertical strip
with the points facing to the right. Label this as Piece
32 (*Fig. 1*).

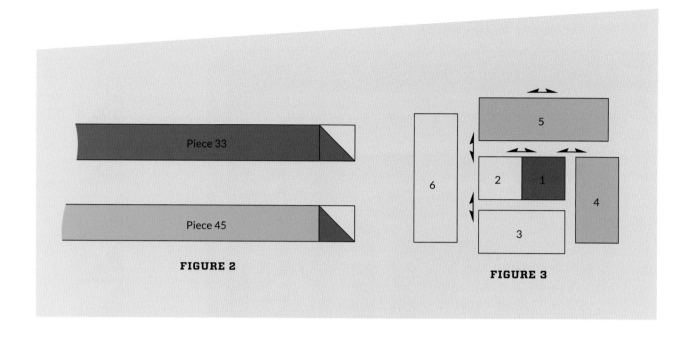

Piece 33

Piece 45

FIGURE 2

5

6

2 1

4

3

FIGURE 3

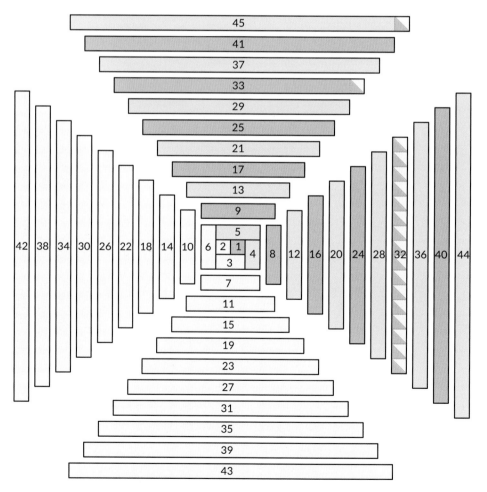

COLORBLOCK ASSEMBLY DIAGRAM

3 Sew one HST to one end of Piece 33 (*Fig. 2*). Rotate one HST and sew it to one end of Piece 45 (*Fig. 2*).

4 Refer to the **Colorblock Assembly Diagram**, following the sewing order as shown. Work counter-clockwise and press seams open as you go. Sew Piece 2 to the left side of Piece 1 (*Fig. 3*). Add pieces 3, 4, 5, and 6 as shown. Continue sewing in numerical order until all pieces are sewn on, ending with Piece 45.

FINISH THE QUILT

1 Trim the selvedges off your backing fabric. Cut two strips 6" × WOF. Cut one of those strips down to 6" × 10" (15 × 25.5 cm) and keep the leftover for another use. Using a ½" (1.3 cm) seam allowance, sew the 6" × 10" (15 × 25.5 cm) strip to the short side of the WOF, then sew the elongated strip to the long side of the main backing fabric.

2 Use your favorite method to layer and baste your quilt top, batting, and backing. Quilt as desired. I chose to quilt in the ditch.

3 Sew together the binding strips end to end diagonally and use your preferred method to bind the quilt.

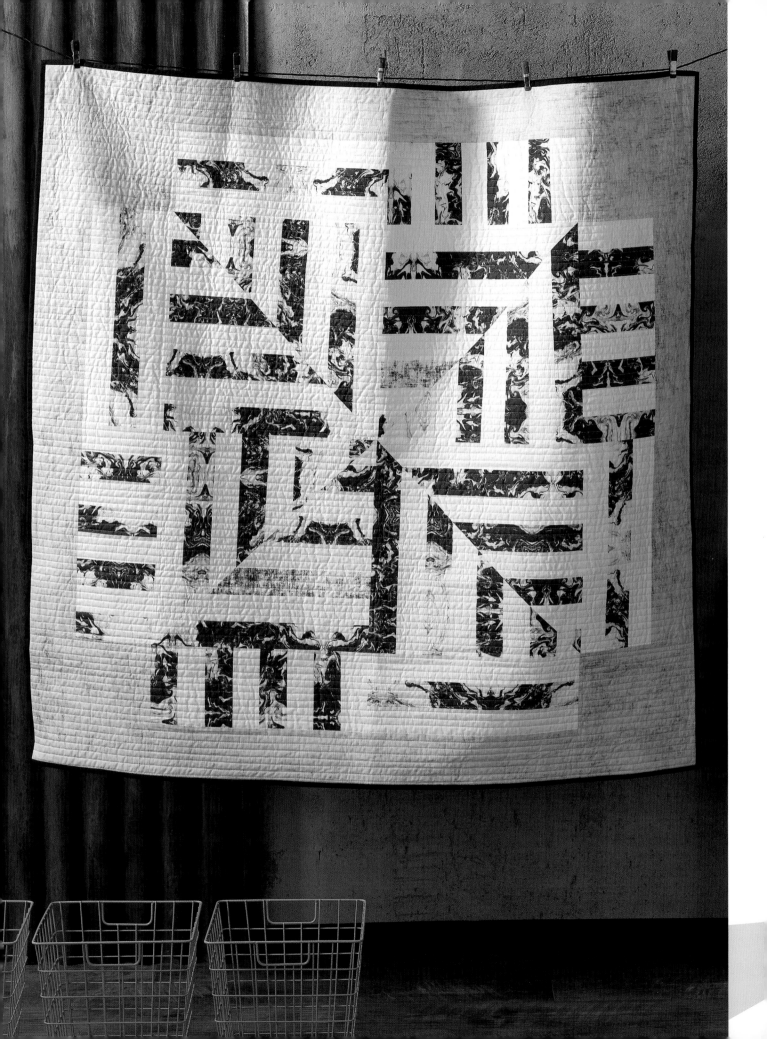

BROOKLYN
quilt

This graphic quilt was inspired by some marble floors I happened to notice. They reminded me of the floors you see in some older apartments in a place like Brooklyn. Although this quilt is made from just two simple blocks, it's made unique by the introduction of strong diagonals that abruptly interrupt the movement in the design. This design can be subtle or striking, depending on the fabrics used.

Finished Size:

52" × 52" (132 × 132 cm)

Materials

Yardage is based on fabric with a usable width of 42" (106.5 cm).

1½ yd (137 cm) light fabric

1⅛ yd (114.5 cm) dark fabric

1 yd (91.5 cm) border fabric

3½ yd (3.2 m) backing fabric

60" × 60" (152.5 × 152.5 cm) piece of batting

½ yd (45.5 cm) binding fabric

Tools

Long acrylic ruler with a 45-degree angle mark

Cutting

WOF = width of fabric

From light fabric, cut:

1 strip 18" × WOF (45.5 cm × WOF) (A & B); subcut into 1 piece 12" × 18" (30.5 × 45.5 cm) and 1 piece 30" × 18" (76 × 45.5 cm)

From the piece 12" × 18" (30.5 × 45.5 cm), subcut 4 pieces 3" × 18" (7.5 × 45.5 cm)

From the piece 30" × 18" (76 × 45.5 cm), subcut 12 pieces 2½" × 18" (6.5 × 45.5 cm)

4 strips 2½" × WOF (6.5 cm × WOF); subcut into 4 pieces 27" × 2½" (68.5 × 6.5 cm) (C)

4 strips 2 ½" × WOF (6.5 cm × WOF); subcut into 8 pieces 18" × 2½" (45.5 × 6.5 cm) (D).

From dark fabric, cut:

1 strip 18" × WOF (45.5 cm × WOF) (A & B); subcut into 1 piece 12" × 18" (30.5 × 45.5 cm) and 1 piece 30" × 18" (76 × 45.5 cm)

From the piece 12" × 18" (30.5 × 45.5 cm), subcut 4 pieces 3" × 18" (7.5 × 45.5 cm)

From the piece 30" × 18" (76 × 45.5 cm), subcut 12 pieces 2½" × 18" (6.5 × 45.5 cm)

4 strips 2½" × WOF (6.5 cm × WOF); subcut into 4 pieces 27" × 2½" (68.5 × 6.5 cm) (C)

2 strips 2½" × WOF (6.5 cm × WOF); subcut into 4 pieces 18" × 2½" (45.5 × 6.5 cm) (D).

From border fabric, cut:

1 strip 10½" × WOF (26.5 cm × WOF); subcut into 4 squares 10½" × 10½" (26.5 × 26.5 cm) (E).

1 strip 18" × 32½" (45.5 × 82.5 cm); subcut into 4 strips 4½" × 32½" (11.5 × 82.5 cm) (F).

From binding fabric, cut:

6 strips 2½" × WOF (6.5 cm × WOF).

BROOKLYN QUILT

MAKE THE BLOCKS

For the quilt center, you will make four identical blocks, then reconfigure them with diagonal seams to create two blocks A and two blocks B. All seams are ¼".

1 Place one light fabric strip 3" × 18" (7.5 × 45.5 cm) right sides together with one dark strip 2½" × 18" (6.5 × 45.5 cm), and sew along the long edge as shown (***Fig. 1***). Add and sew on additional three light strips 2½" × 18" (6.5 × 45.5 cm) and two dark strips 2½" × 18" (6.5 × 45.5 cm), alternating the colors. Finally, sew on one dark strip 3" × 18" (7.5 × 45.5 cm). Press. This completes one block.

2 Repeat Step 1 to make a total of four striped blocks. Double check with an acrylic ruler to make sure your stripes are even and straight (***Fig 2***). Trim the blocks to 17½" × 17½" (44.5 × 44.5 cm), making sure to keep consistent seam allowances.

3 Place two of the blocks right sides together so the light strips line up with the dark strips and vice versa (***Fig. 3***).

4 Using an acrylic ruler, draw a line with a fabric marker from one corner to the other. Mark lines a scant ¼" (6 mm) on either side of this line (***Figs. 4 and 5***). Fold the top back as shown (***Fig. 6***) (page 40) to make sure seams line up, and pin.

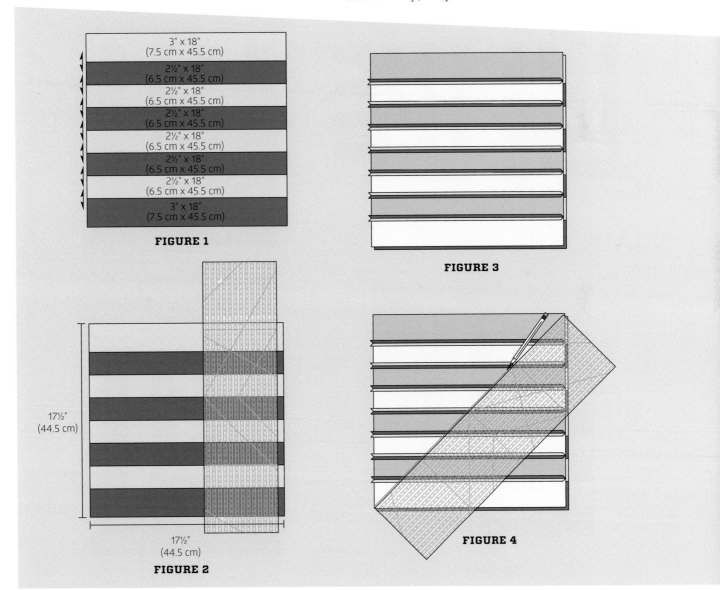

3" x 18"
(7.5 cm x 45.5 cm)

2½" x 18"
(6.5 cm x 45.5 cm)

2½" x 18"
(6.5 cm x 45.5 cm)

2½" x 18"
(6.5 cm x 45.5 cm)

2½" x 18"
(6.5 cm x 45.5 cm)

2½" x 18"
(6.5 cm x 45.5 cm)

2½" x 18"
(6.5 cm x 45.5 cm)

3" x 18"
(7.5 cm x 45.5 cm)

FIGURE 1

FIGURE 3

17½"
(44.5 cm)

17½"
(44.5 cm)

FIGURE 2

FIGURE 4

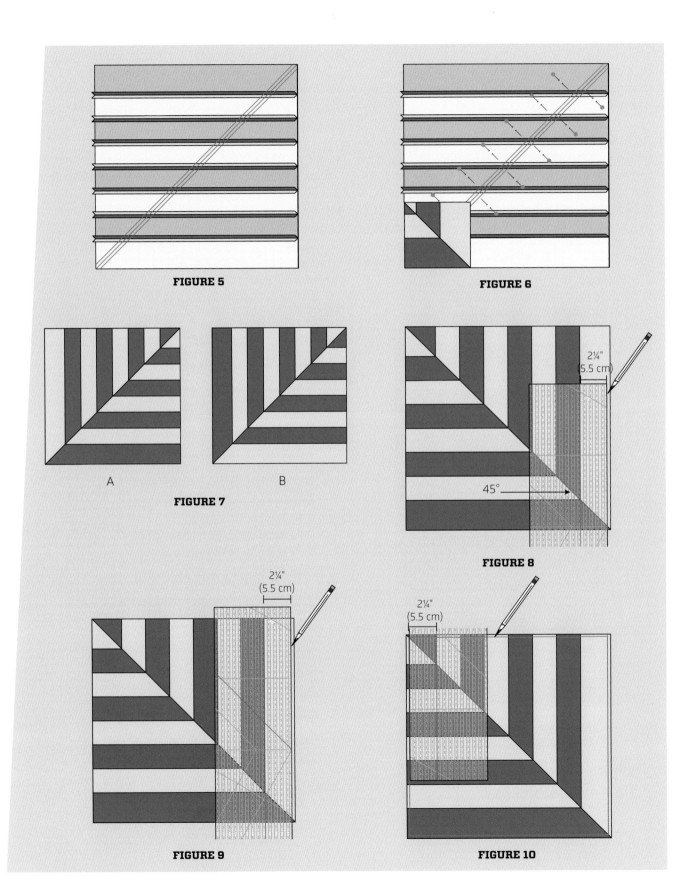

FIGURE 5

FIGURE 6

A   B

FIGURE 7

2¼"
(5.5 cm)

45°

FIGURE 8

2¼"
(5.5 cm)

FIGURE 9

2¼"
(5.5 cm)

FIGURE 10

5 Sew carefully along the two outside lines. Open up both sides to check that all the seams are lined up. If not, use a seam ripper to open the areas that are off, shift them carefully into place, and re-sew them back in the correct position.

6 Cut apart along the middle line. Press the seams open. You now have one block A and one block B (*Fig. 7*).

7 Repeat Steps 3 to 6 for the other two blocks, and make another A/B set for a total of two blocks each of A and B.

SQUARE UP THE BLOCKS

1 Place a block right side up. Place an acrylic ruler on top with the 45-degree angle following the diagonal in the block. Keeping it lined up, have the 2¼" (5.5 cm) mark lined up with the two long striped seam lines (*Fig. 8*). Mark with a fabric marker along the edges of the ruler. Move the ruler if necessary to draw your lines across the block (*Fig. 9*).

2 Flip the ruler around to the other corner, and line up the 45-degree angle with the diagonal. Measure and mark a 2½" (6.5 cm) half-square triangle (HST) in the corner (*Fig. 10*). Connect all lines to make a block 16½" × 16½" (42 × 42 cm).

3 Once all four sides are marked, trim away the excess. Repeat steps 1 to 3 for the other blocks.

Spotlight

This simple design is really flexible! You can play with it to get a variety of effects, depending on which way you orient the four blocks.

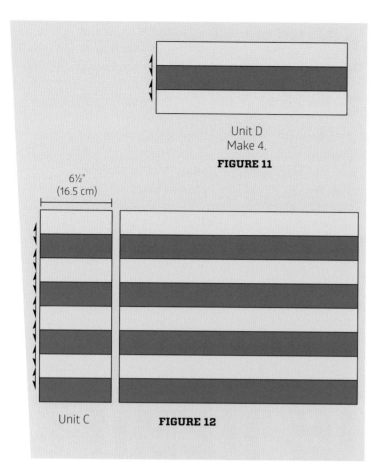

Unit D
Make 4.
FIGURE 11

6½"
(16.5 cm)

Unit C

FIGURE 12

MAKE UNITS C & D

*As shown in the **Brooklyn Assembly Diagram** (page 43, the borders of the quilt are made with units C and D—which are pieced—and plain background fabric units E and F.*

1 To make Unit D, sew together two light fabric strips 2½" × 16½" (6.5 × 42 cm) and one dark fabric strip 2½" × 16½" (6.5 × 42 cm), with the dark strip in the middle (**Fig. 11**). Make four units. Press the seams open.

2 To make Unit C, sew together four light strips 2½" × 27" (6.5 × 68.5 cm) and four dark strips 2½" × 27" (6.5 × 68.5 cm), starting with the light strip and alternating the colors (**Fig. 11**). Press the seams open.

3 Trim a little off one side of the unit to make it square. From this, cut four strips 6½" (16.5 cm) (**Fig. 12**).

ASSEMBLE THE QUILT TOP

*Refer to the **Brooklyn Assembly Diagram** as you complete the following steps.*

1 To assemble the quilt center, place one Block B right side up with the small HST in the upper left corner. Place the other B block right side down with the small HST in the lower right-hand corner. Pin in place and sew along the right side. Press the seam open.

2 Place one Block A right side up with the small HST in the upper right corner. Place the other A block right side down with the small HST in the lower left corner. Pin in place and sew along the right side. Press the seam open.

3 Sew the two pieces together with B on top and A on bottom (**Fig. 13**). Press the seam open.

4 Referring to the Brooklyn Assembly Diagram, sew the striped border units and the border fabric squares and strips. Sew the top and bottom to the quilt center first, then sew on the sides. Press.

> ### TIP
> Precision and consistency are particularly important in making this quilt top. When you are sewing long strips, the seams can get distorted. To help prevent this, try sewing on each strip in the opposite direction from the previous one.

FINISH THE QUILT

1 Cut the backing fabric in half lengthwise. Sew the two pieces together along the longest sides using a ½" (1.3 cm) seam. You will now have a 63" × 83" (160 × 211 cm) back. Press the seam open.

2 Use your favorite method to layer and baste your quilt top, batting, and backing. Quilt as desired. I kept it simple, with narrowly spaced parallel quilting across the entire quilt top. However, this quilt also lends itself to amazing possibilities with geometric quilting.

3 Sew the binding strips together end to end diagonally and use your preferred method to bind the quilt.

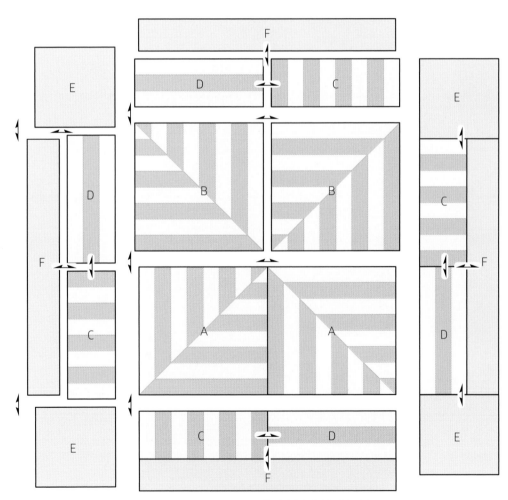

BROOKLYN ASSEMBLY DIAGRAM

STONES

quilt

Make this small project to showcase a few of your favorite prints or solids while reducing your scrap bin at the same time. This quilt also affords a nice opportunity to practice fussy cutting and improvisational piecing. Expand this project by using it as a template for a modern I Spy quilt, or for a color theory exploration. Once you learn how to piece the "stones" blocks, you can easily adjust their size. This project truly lets your imagination run free.

Finished Size:

16" × 28" (40.5 × 71 cm)

Materials

Yardage is based on fabric with a usable width of 42" (106.5 cm), unless otherwise noted.

15 squares 4" × 4" (10 × 10 cm) of various prints*

Strips of fabric 5"–6" (12.5–15 cm) long in various widths for decoration, optional

1 yd (91.5 cm) background fabric

24" × 36" (61 × 91.5 cm) piece of batting

24" × 36" (61 × 91.5 cm) piece of backing fabric

1 fat quarter (45.5 × 56 cm) for binding

STONES QUILT

Tools

Washable fabric marking pen

Cutting

WOF= width of fabric

From background fabric, cut:

8 strips 2½" × WOF (6.5 cm × WOF); subcut into 60 strips 2½" × 5" (6.5 × 12.5 cm)

3 strips 1½" × WOF (3.8 cm × WOF); subcut into 10 strips 1½" × 4" (3.8 × 10 cm), and 4 strips 1½" × 13" (3.8 × 33 cm)

2 strips 2" × WOF (5 cm × WOF); trim each strip to 2" × 22" (5 × 56 cm)

1 strip 3¾" WOF (9.5 cm × WOF); subcut into 2 strips 3¾" × 16" (9.5 × 40.5 cm).

From binding fabric, cut:

5 strips 2½" × 21" (6.5 × 53.5 cm).

> ### TIP
>
> Some of the "stones" in this quilt have decorative strips of a contrasting fabric, while others are cut as whole shapes from a single fabric. Inserting strips in any or all of the stones is optional.
>
> *If you want to add a decorative strip to a stone, cut the square for that stone to 4¼" × 4¼" (11.5 × 11.5 cm).*

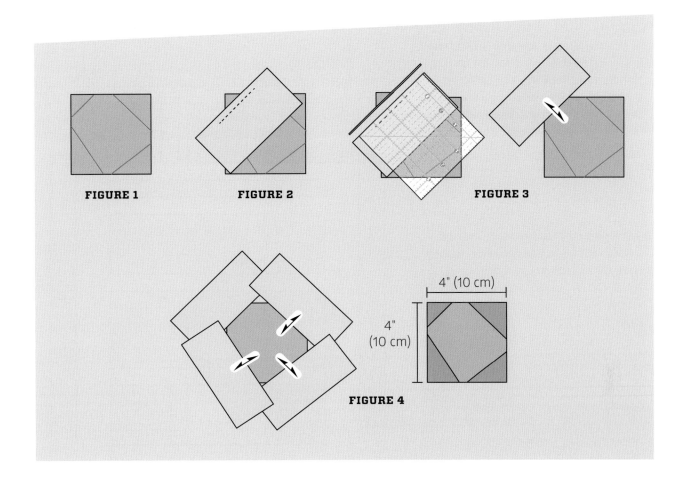

FIGURE 1

FIGURE 2

FIGURE 3

4" (10 cm)

4"
(10 cm)

FIGURE 4

MAKE THE BLOCKS

To add an optional decorative strip to one or more stones, refer to **My Method: Inserting Decorative Strips,** *page 49.*

1 Lay out the fifteen stone fabric squares in the order you like. Using a washable fabric marker and a ruler, draw lines to create random angles (*Fig. 1*). This will give you a general idea of the overall look of your stones when you are finished.

2 Place one square right side up, and place one piece of background fabric 2½" × 5" (6.5 × 12.5 cm) right side down on top, extending about ¼" (6 mm) over the marked line in one corner. Using the edge of the background fabric as a seam guide, sew a ¼" (6 mm) seam (*Fig. 2*). It's okay if your seam line is not directly on the marked line; that line is just a general guide to show you the angle. Repeat with all fifteen stones. Chain piecing works well here (see Chain Piecing, page 16).

3 On each sewn stone piece, line up the ¼" (6 mm) mark of a ruler along the seam line and trim off the excess fabric (*Fig. 3*). Press the seams open.

4 Repeat steps 1 to 3 for the second corner of each stone piece. Repeat for the third and fourth corners (*Fig. 4*). Trim all the stone blocks to 4" × 4" (10 × 10 cm). If you would like a rounder stone, cut extra pieces 2 ½" × 5"(6.5 × 12.5 cm) and use less of an angle.

ASSEMBLE THE QUILT TOP

1 Refer to the **Stones Assembly Diagram** to sew together the top row. Sew vertical sashing strips of background fabric 1½" × 4" (3.8 × 10 cm) between two stone blocks. Sew on the third stone block. Press. Repeat to make a total of five rows.

2 Sew a horizontal sashing strip of background fabric 1½" × 13" (3.8 × 33 cm) to the bottom of rows 1 to 4. Press.

3 Sew together all the rows and sashings, ending with the last row of stone blocks. Press. Sew a background fabric strip 2" × 22" (5 × 56 cm) to each side. Sew a strip 3¾" × 16" (9.5 × 40.5 cm) to the top and bottom. Press.

FINISH THE QUILT

1 Use your favorite method to layer and baste your quilt top, batting, and backing.

2 Quilt as desired. I chose to echo-quilt around the stones, continuing the contours on the background at the quilt top and bottom.

3 Sew together the binding strips end to end diagonally and use your preferred method to bind the quilt.

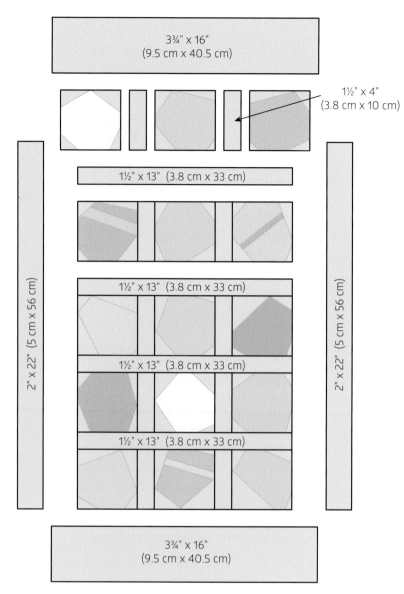

STONES ASSEMBLY DIAGRAM

TIP

To turn this light-weight little quilt into a wall hanging, I used appliqué pins. They are easy to put in the wall, and they leave the tiniest marks in both the quilt and the wall.

My Method: Inserting Decorative Strips

Lay a square of stone fabric 4¼" × 4¼" (11.5 × 11.5 cm) right side up. Place a strip of contrasting fabric 5"–6" (12.5–15 cm) long on top, right side down, positioned at any angle you want. Sew one edge of the strip using a ¼" (6 mm) seam.

Trim off the stone fabric, flip it right side down as shown, and sew the stone fabric you just trimmed off back onto the other side. Press the seams open. Lock or backstitch at the start and end of stitching.

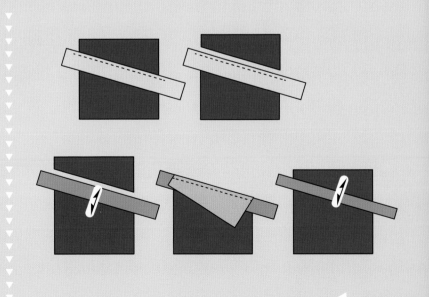

SEQUOIA

quilt

#sequoiaquilt

This quilt unites high style with functionality. Sequoias are known for their height and longevity, and for their bold, beautiful form. Here, triangle shapes and colors work together in harmony to create a bold quilt design also worthy of passing down to future generations. Despite its complex look, this design is simple to make using half-square triangles cut from solid fabrics.

Finished Size:

56" × 70" (142 × 178 cm)

Materials

Yardage is based on fabric with a usable width of 42" (106.5 cm).

2¼ yd (2.1 m) white fabric

5/8 yd (66.5 cm) black fabric

1 yd (91.5 cm) gray fabric

1 yd (91.5 cm) green fabric

3½ yd (3.2 m) backing fabric

60" × 74" (152.5 × 188 cm) piece of batting

½ yd (45.5 cm) binding fabric

SEQUOIA QUILT

Cutting

WOF= width of fabric

From white fabric, cut:
7 strips 6½" × WOF (16.5 cm × WOF); subcut into 42 squares 6½" × 6½" (16.5 × 16.5 cm) and 5 squares 4" × 4" (10 cm × 10 cm).

7 strips 4" × WOF (10 cm × WOF); subcut into 71 squares 4" × 4" (10 × 10 cm).

From black fabric, cut:
2 strips 6½" × WOF (16.5 cm × WOF); subcut into 10 squares 6½" × 6½" (16.5 × 16.5 cm).

3 strips 4" × WOF (10 cm × WOF); subcut into 24 squares 4" × 4" (10 × 10 cm).

From gray fabric, cut:
4 strips 6½" × WOF (16.5 cm × WOF); subcut into 21 squares 6½" × 6½" (16.5 × 16.5 cm).

2 strips 4" × WOF (10 cm × WOF); subcut into 16 squares 4" × 4" (10 × 10 cm).

From green fabric, cut:
3 strips 6½" × WOF (16.5 cm × WOF); subcut into 15 squares 6½" × 6½" (16.5 × 16.5 cm).

3 strips 4" × WOF (10 cm × WOF); subcut into 28 squares 4" × 4" (10 × 10 cm).

From binding fabric, cut:
7 strips 2½" × WOF (6.5 cm × WOF).

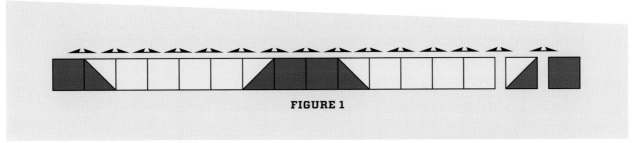

FIGURE 1

ASSEMBLE THE QUILT TOP

All seams are ¼" (6 mm).

1 Place the squares 6½" × 6½" (16.5 × 16.5 cm) right sides together in pairs, in the following color combinations:

→ 8 pairs black/white

→ 21 pairs gray/white

→ 13 pairs green/white

→ 2 pairs green/black

2 Refer to *My Method: Making Half-Square Triangles* (page 27) and use the Four units at a time method to make HSTs from the paired squares. Trim all the units to 4" × 4" (10 × 10 cm). You will have a total of thirty-two black/white, eighty-four gray/white, fifty-two green/white, and eight green/black HSTs.

3 This quilt has twenty rows, each made up of a total of sixteen HST units and plain squares 4" × 4" (10 × 10 cm). Refer to the *Sequoia Assembly Diagram* (page 54) for placement of the colors. Starting with the top and working from left to right, sew the units together to create the top row (*Fig. 1*). Press. Sew all twenty rows.

4 Starting from the top and working your way down, sew the rows together as shown in the *Sequoia Assembly Diagram*. Make sure to line up your seams. Press.

SEQUOIA ASSEMBLY DIAGRAM

FINISH THE QUILT

1 Trim the selvedges off the backing fabric. Cut the fabric in half to yield two pieces 63" (160 cm) × WOF. Sew the pieces together along the 63" (160 cm) edges, using a ½" (1.3 cm) seam allowance. Press the seam open.

2 Use your favorite method to layer and baste your quilt top, batting, and backing. Quilt as desired. To play up the diagonal lines of the design, I did a crosshatch design.

3 Sew together the binding strips end to end diagonally and use your preferred method to bind the quilt.

WAYWARD
quilt

This improvisational quilt is great for beginners because very little precision is needed in making the wonky triangle blocks that form the design. Let your creative side show by playing around with the layout to create your own pattern. You can also customize this quilt by adding more or fewer triangles and by adjusting the border sizes. For this project, you will get to practice wonky piecing!

Finished Size:

48½" × 60½" (123 × 153.5 cm)

Materials

Yardage is based on fabric with a usable width of 42" (106.5 cm), unless otherwise noted.

3 different fat quarters or ⅛ yards (11.5 cm) of fabric for the triangles*

3¼ yd (3 m) background fabric

3 yd (2.75 m) backing fabric

52" × 64" (132 × 162.5 cm) batting

½ yd (45.5 cm) binding fabric

*For the look pictured, choose a medium and dark value of one color, plus a light contrasting color.

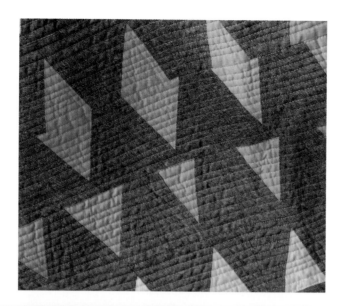

Cutting

WOF= width of fabric

From each of the fat quarters, cut:
1 strip 4¼" × 21" (11.5 × 53.5 cm).

From background fabric, cut:
21 strips 3" × WOF (7.5 cm × WOF);
subcut into 162 pieces 3" × 5½"
(7.5 × 14 cm)

2 pieces 6½" × 36½" (16.5 × 92.5 cm)

1 piece 18½" × 48½" (47 × 123 cm)

1 piece 6½" × 48½" (16.5 × 123 cm).

From binding fabric, cut:
6 strips 2½" × WOF (6.5 cm × WOF).

WAYWARD QUILT

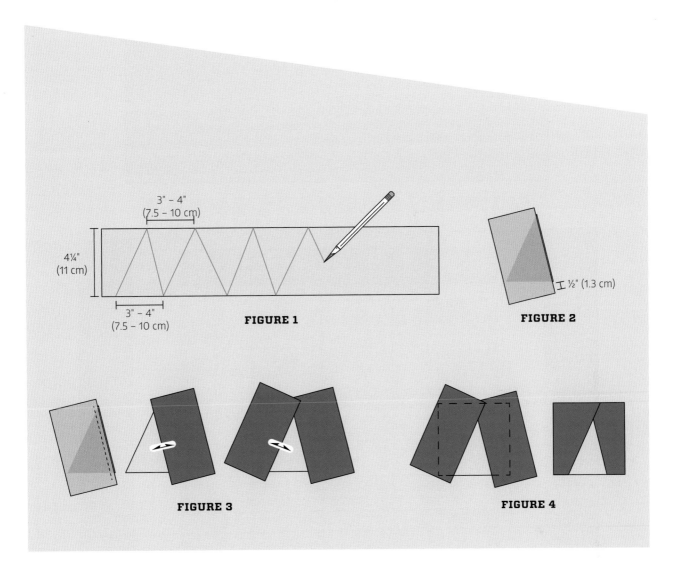

3" – 4"
(7.5 – 10 cm)

4¼"
(11 cm)

3" – 4"
(7.5 – 10 cm)

FIGURE 1

½" (1.3 cm)

FIGURE 2

FIGURE 3

FIGURE 4

MAKE THE BLOCKS

This quilt has eighty-one triangle blocks. Use a ¼" (6 mm) seam allowance.

1 To make the triangles, use a washable fabric marker and ruler to draw triangles along each fat quarter strip as shown (**Fig. 1**). For a wonky look, vary the triangle bases from 3"–4" (7.5–10 cm) wide.

2 Cut out the triangles. I cut twenty-six light peach triangles, thirty-two dark peach triangles, and twenty-three cream triangles, for a total of eighty-one triangles. But you can choose how many of each color you want, as long as you end up with a total of eighty-one triangles.

3 To create a triangle block, lay one triangle right side up and position one background piece 3" × 5½" (7.5 × 15 cm) right side down on top, as shown (**Fig. 2**). Make sure the background piece extends ½" (1.3 cm) beyond the triangle base. Sew along the triangle edge (**Fig. 3**). Trim the seam allowances down to ¼" (6 mm). Press the seam open. Repeat for the other side of the triangle. Press the seam open. Repeat to make a total of eighty-one triangle blocks.

4 Press the blocks and trim each to 4½" × 4½" (11.5 × 11.5 cm) (**Fig. 4**).

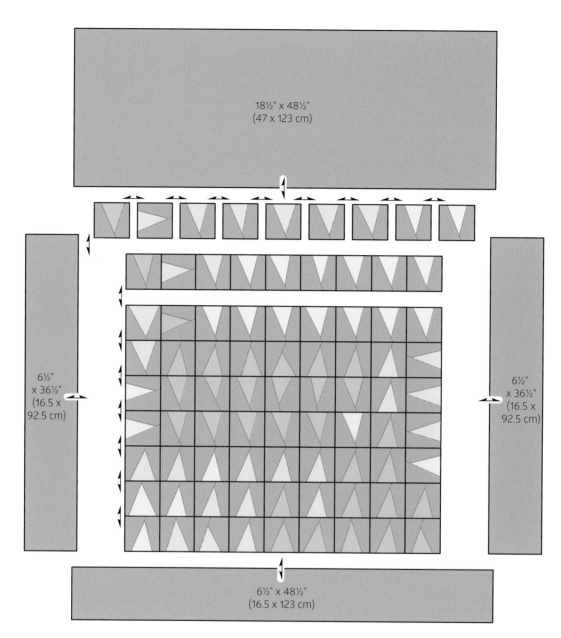

18½" x 48½"
(47 x 123 cm)

6½"
x 36½"
(16.5 x
92.5 cm)

6½"
x 36½"
(16.5 x
92.5 cm)

6½" x 48½"
(16.5 x 123 cm)

WAYWARD ASSEMBLY DIAGRAM

ASSEMBLE THE QUILT TOP

1 Refer to the **Wayward Assembly Diagram** to lay out your eighty-one triangle blocks in the order pictured, or in a manner that is pleasing to you. In this example, I played with the triangles' orientation; some point upward, some downward, and a few sideways. Notice also the arrangement of the colors. You can achieve different effects by rearranging your three colors.

2 Sew together nine blocks to create a row. Repeat to sew nine rows total. Press. Sew the rows together, pressing the seams open, to create the quilt center.

3 Sew a background piece 6½" × 36½" (16.5 × 92.5 cm) to each side of the quilt center.

4 Sew the background piece 6½" × 48½" (16.5 × 123 cm) to the bottom, and sew the background piece 18½" × 48½" (47 × 123 cm) to the top. Press.

FINISH THE QUILT

1 Trim the selvedges from the backing fabric, and cut two strips 15" × WOF (38 cm × WOF). Subcut one strip 28" (71 cm). Sew together the two strips using a ½" (1.3 cm) seam allowance. Press the seam open.

2 Sew the long strip to the remainder of the backing fabric along its longest side, again using a ½" (1.3 cm) seam. Press the seam open.

3 Use your favorite method to layer and baste your quilt top, batting, and backing. Quilt as desired. To fill in the negative background space and add textural interest, I did straight-line quilting in narrowly spaced parallel lines.

4 Sew together the binding strips end to end diagonally, and use your preferred method to bind the quilt.

SPLIT DECISION
mini quilt

This fun little quilt is a good introduction to paper piecing. The Flying Geese are going in different directions, giving this quilt lots of movement. And the "split" Flying Geese made up of print fabric in two different colorways add interest. I used a text-printed background fabric to create a subtle but lively background around the vivid colors of the Flying Geese. This design will work really well in a variety of different color and fabric choices.

Finished Size:
20½" × 20½" (52 × 52 cm)

Materials
Yardage is based on fabric with a usable width of 42" (106.5 cm), unless otherwise noted.

Scraps in 8 coordinating solid colors for the Flying Geese units

Scraps in 2 prints for the split Flying Geese units

Scrap at least 10" × 4" (25.5 × 10 cm) for the center

¾ yd (68.5 cm) background fabric

1 yd (91.5 cm) backing fabric

24" × 24" (61 × 61 cm) piece of batting

1 fat quarter of binding fabric

Tools

Paper for paper piecing

4 copies of Split Decision template patterns A, B, C, D, E, and F (pages 144–147)

Blue painter's tape or masking tape

Washable glue for glue basting

Cutting

WOF = width of fabric

From Flying Geese solids:
For Template A/B, cut:

4 pieces 2½" × 2" (6.5 × 5 cm) (Piece 8)

12 pieces 2½" × 3½" (6.5 × 9 cm) (Pieces 2, 4, and 6).

SPLIT DECISION MINI QUILT

For Template C/D, cut:
4 pieces 2½" × 4" (6.5 × 10 cm) (Piece 24) from one chosen color.

For Template E/F, cut:
4 pieces 2½" × 2" (6.5 × 5 cm) (Piece 8)

12 pieces 2½" × 3½" (6.5 × 9 cm) (Pieces 2, 4, and 6).

From Flying Geese prints:
For Template C/D, cut:

32 pieces 2½" × 4" (6.5 × 10 cm) in your chosen colors (Pieces 3, 6, 9, 12, 15, 18, 21).

From background fabric:
For Templates A/B & E/F, cut and split into 4 stacks of 2 each:

1 strip 9½" × 24" (24 × 61 cm); subcut into eight strips 3" × 9½" (7.5 × 24 cm) (Piece 1)

1 strip 7" × 24" (18 × 61 cm); subcut into eight strips 3" × 7" (7.5 × 18 cm) (Piece 3)

1 strip 5" × 24" (12.5 × 61 cm); subcut into eight strips 3" × 5" (7.5 × 12.5 cm) (Piece 5)

1 strip 2" × 24" (5 × 61 cm); subcut into eight strips 3" × 2" (7.5 × 5 cm) (Piece 7)

1 strip 2½" × 20" (6.5 × 51 cm); subcut into eight squares 2½" × 2½" (6.5 × 6.5 cm) (Piece 9).

For Template C/D, cut:
3 strips 3½" × WOF (9 cm × WOF); subcut into 56 strips 2" × 3½₁₂" (5 × 7.8 cm) (Pieces 4, 5, 7, 8, 10, 11, 13, 14, 16, 17, 19, 20, 22, 23)

1 strip 4" × 10"(6.5 × 25.5 cm); subcut into 4 strips 2½" × 4" (6.5 × 10 cm) (Piece 2).

From center fabric, cut:
4 pieces 2½" × 4" (6.5 × 10 cm) (for Template C/D, Piece 1).

From binding fabric, cut:
2 strips 2½" × WOF (6.5 cm × WOF).

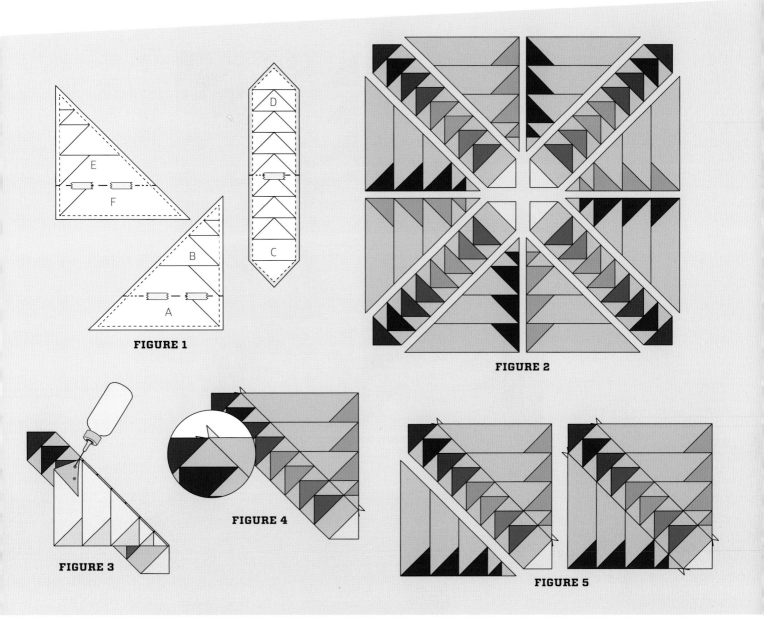

FIGURE 1

FIGURE 2

FIGURE 3

FIGURE 4

FIGURE 5

MAKE THE BLOCKS

This quilt has four blocks. All seams are ¼" (6 mm).

1 Refer to **My Method: Paper Piecing** (page 67) to make and cut out four copies each of templates A, B, C, D, E, and F. Tape together templates A to B, C to D, and E to F as shown (**Fig. 1**).

2 Sew down all the template pieces. Remember to sew them in numerical order.

3 When finished, lay out the pieces right sides up, as shown (**Fig. 2**).

4 Remove the paper along the seams. Place one set of A/B and C/D right sides together, line up the seams, and glue baste (**Fig. 3**).

5 Sew a ¼" (6 mm) seam, and press open. There will be ½" (1.3 cm) dog ears on either side (**Fig. 4**).

6 Sew one set E/F to the other side of A/B/C/D as shown (**Fig. 5**). Press the seam open.

7 Repeat steps 3–5 for the remaining pieces to make a total of four blocks.

SPLIT DECISION ASSMBLY DIAGRAM

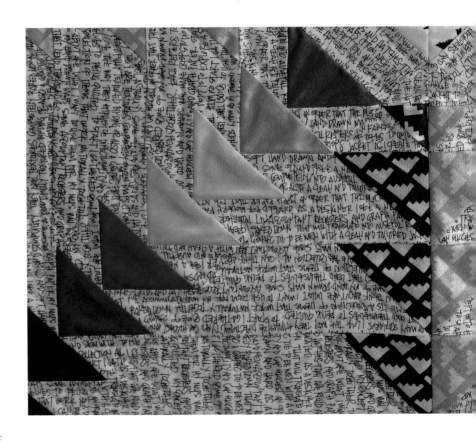

ASSEMBLE THE QUILT TOP

1 Refer to the **Split Decision Assembly Diagram** to arrange the four blocks. Sew two finished blocks together with the "split" Flying Geese in the center as shown. Press the seam open. Repeat for the other two blocks.

2 Sew the two units together and press the seams open.

FINISH THE QUILT

1 Use your favorite method to layer and baste your quilt top, batting, and backing. Quilt as desired. I did very simple outline quilting.

2 Sew together the binding strips end to end diagonally, and use your preferred method to bind the quilt.

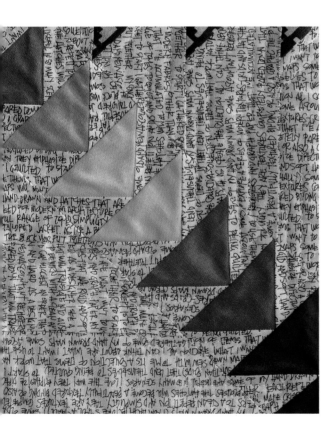

My Method: Paper Piecing

In a nutshell, paper piecing, also called foundation piecing, starts with a paper template representing a block or a part of a block. The shapes within the block are marked with sewing lines. Rough-cut pieces of fabric are placed on the template, overlapping the lines. The sections within the template are numbered, and you sew them in numerical order, sewing through both paper and fabric. (Because the fabric pieces must be cut slightly larger than the finished shapes, there is some fabric waste. This is necessary because the fabric is flipped over after sewing, and this ensures all edges will be covered when sewn together.)

Most approaches to paper piecing instruct you to sew on the printed side of the paper template. Although this is the traditional way, I always found myself getting confused because this method reverses the pattern. (Because you position the fabrics right side down to the back side of the printed template and sew on the front side, the finished block's direction is reversed from what you see printed on the template.) I ended up with a lot of orphan blocks.

My brain works in such a way that I want my finished product to look just like what I see at the beginning. So after photocopying a template pattern onto paper, I trace the lines on the back of the paper and sew the fabric to the front side. It requires an extra step, but it takes the guesswork out of the project, and the template is never reversed. Plus, no more orphan blocks.

WHAT YOU'LL NEED

Note: I save old but salvageable sewing machine needles for paper piecing instead of using sharp new needles.

→ Plain computer or copy paper
→ Scissors for cutting paper
→ Pen
→ Sewing pins
→ Sharp fabric scissors or a rotary cutter and mat
→ Small clear acrylic ruler
→ Light source next to your sewing machine, such as a window or lamp
→ Blue painter's tape or masking tape
→ Iron
→ Fabrics cut as indicated in the pattern you are using

continued on next page

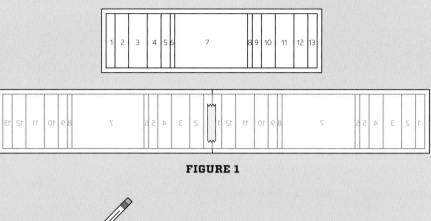

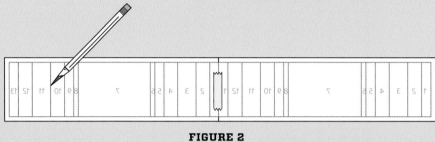

FIGURE 1

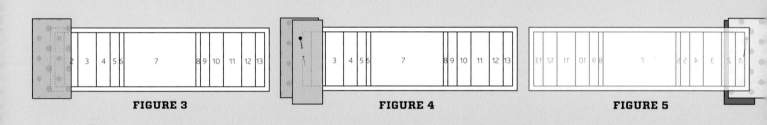

FIGURE 2

FIGURE 3   **FIGURE 4**   **FIGURE 5**

HERE'S HOW

All seams will be trimmed to leave a ¼" (6 mm) seam allowance.

1 Photocopy the template patterns and cut out the paper templates with paper scissors, following the outer lines (*Fig. 1*). If the templates are in two or three pieces that need to be joined, align and tape them together after cutting out.

2 Tape the template to a window or hold it up to another light source, and carefully trace the stitching lines on the backside with a pen (*Fig. 2*). There is no need to trace the seam allowances. Add the piece numbers to the back of the template. You will sew all the fabric pieces on in numerical order.

3 Place your template with the original printed side up. Place the fabric for Piece 1 right side up. This fabric should extend past the edges of Piece 1 on all sides and extend at least ¼" (6 mm) over the seam line between pieces 1 and 2 (*Fig. 3*).

4 Place the fabric for Piece 2 right side down and over Piece 1. This piece should extend at least ¼" (6 mm) over the seam lines for Pieces 1 and 2 (*Fig 4*). (For clarity in this tutorial, the red dotted line represents the line you will sew when you flip the paper over. As you can see, there is at least ¼" (6 mm) of fabric extending past the red line to the right. The black dotted line is the outline of the paper template underneath the fabric.) Pin into place. Hold the fabric and paper up to a light source. You should be able to see the outlines of the fabrics and paper, which will help you ensure that they extend beyond the sewing lines (*Fig 5*).

5 Flip the template over to the side you marked with your pen. Reduce your stitch length to 1.5 mm. (A smaller stitch will allow easier removal of the paper after sewing.) Stitch along the first line, backstitching at the start and finish (*Fig. 6*). Flip the template over and fold the fabric back to its right side. Double check that it does cover all of Piece 2 and the seams (*Fig. 7*).

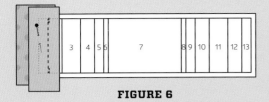

FIGURE 6

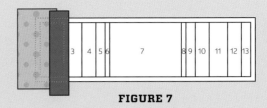

FIGURE 7

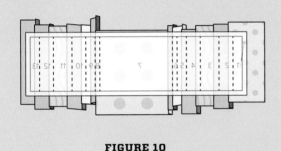

FIGURE 8

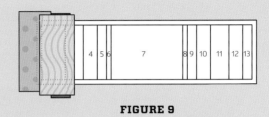

FIGURE 9

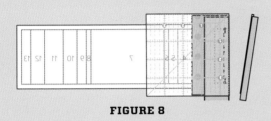

FIGURE 10

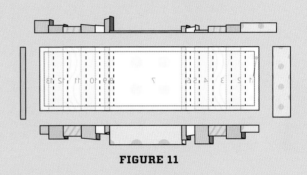

FIGURE 11

6 Fold the fabric and paper away from the seam. Put it on a cutting mat and place an acrylic ruler on top, aligning the ¼" (6 mm) mark along the seam. Trim away any excess (*Fig. 8*).

7 Fold the paper back into place with the right side of Piece 2 showing. Press with a hot iron. Place the fabric for Piece 3 right side down as you did for the second piece in Step 4 (*Fig. 9*). Make sure the fabric extends past the seam line and edges of the paper, and double check using a light source. Repeat steps 4 to 7.

8 Keep adding pieces and sewing until you've completed all the numbers. When you are finished, you should end up with something like this (*Fig. 10*). Place the edge of an acrylic ruler along the edge of the paper. Trim away excess fabric from all sides (*Fig. 11*).

9 When it's time to sew paper-pieced units together or to incorporate them into a block, carefully tear away the paper along the seam that is to be sewn. This will eliminate any need to remove tiny strips of paper later. After the piece has been sewn and you're completely finished, tear the rest of the paper out.

TIP

Some people find it helpful to quickly color in pieces that coordinate with the fabric they are using to serve as general guide while sewing.

CITRUS

quilt

This quilt design is an abstract adaptation of the pockets of citrus fruit, cut in half horizontally. It is a fun and playful design that can look very different depending on the fabrics you choose for the fruit motifs—pastels or brights, prints or solids. The sharp angles in this pattern create movement and lots of visual interest. To ensure neat, accurate angles within the citrus motifs, this design calls for paper piecing.

Finished Size:

70" × 80" (178 × 203 cm)

Note: For this project, it is necessary to prewash all of your fabric in order to preshrink your cottons. The circles are appliquéd onto the quilt top, and they may pucker if not prewashed.

Materials

Yardage is based on fabric with a usable width of 42" (106.5 cm), unless otherwise noted.

14 fat quarters 18" × 22" (45.5 × 56 cm) of solids in a variety of colors (I used blues, greens, oranges, yellows, and pinks, as well as white, gray, and black)

⅜ yd (34.5 cm) white background fabric

⅝ yd (57 cm) light gray background fabric

3½ yd (3.2 m) dark gray background fabric

3 yd (2.75 m) lightweight stabilizer (I used Pellon Wash-N-Gone 541, which is water soluble)

5 yd (4.6 m) backing fabric

78" × 88" (199 × 223.5 cm) piece of batting

¾ yd (68.5 cm) binding fabric

Tools

Paper for paper piecing

Citrus Template Patterns A, B, C, and D (pages 148–151)

Cutting

WOF = width of fabric

From each fat quarter, cut:
3 strips 6" × 22" (15 × 56 cm) along the 18" (45.5 cm) side, for a total of 42 strips.

From white background fabric, cut:
1 strip 10½" × WOF (26.5 cm × WOF); subcut into 2 squares 10½" × 10½" (26.5 × 26.5 cm) (Piece F)

1 strip 2¾" × 20½" (7 × 52 cm) (Piece A)

2 strips 5½" × 10½" (14 × 26.5 cm) (Pieces I and K).

From light gray background fabric, cut:
2 strips 10½" × WOF (26.5 cm × WOF); subcut into 6 squares 10½" × 10½" (26.5 × 26.5 cm) (F)

1 square 10½" × 10½" (26.5 × 26.5 cm) (G)

1 piece 5½" × 10½" (14 × 26.5 cm) (H).

From dark gray background fabric, cut:
1 piece 35½" × WOF (90 cm × WOF); subcut into: 1 piece 35½" × 20½" (90 × 52 cm) (C), and 2 pieces 35½" × 10½" (90 × 26.5 cm) (M and N)

1 piece 25½" × WOF (65 cm × WOF); subcut into 2 pieces 25½" × 20½" (65 × 52 cm) (D and E)

1 piece 33" × WOF (84 cm × WOF); subcut into 1 piece 20½" × 33" (52 × 84 cm) (B), and 6 squares 10½" × 10½" (26.5 × 26.5 cm) (F)

2 pieces 10½" × WOF (26.5 × WOF); subcut into 6 squares 10½" × 10½" (26.5 × 26.5 cm) (F), and 1 piece 5½" × 10½" (14 × 26.5 cm) (J)

1 piece 20½" × 10½" (52 × 26.5 cm) (L).

From binding fabric, cut:
8 strips 2½" × WOF (6.5 cm × WOF).

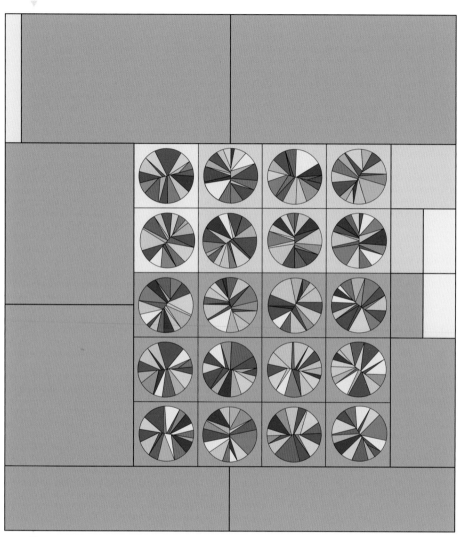

CITRUS QUILT

TIP

To make quicker work of cutting strips from the fat quarters, you can stack all fourteen fat quarters, aligning the edges. It's okay if some of the pieces are a little off, but you want things as even and neat as possible. Along the 18" (45.5 cm) side, cut three strips 6" × 22" (15 × 56 cm) through all layers. (You'll need a very sharp rotary cutter!) If your rotary cutter cannot handle fourteen layers at a time, you can divide them up.

MAKE THE BLOCKS

The finished circles will be lined with stabilizer, so there will be no raw edges on the perimeters.

1 Refer to ***My Method: Paper Piecing*** (page 67) to make and cut out ten each of Citrus Templates A, B, C, and D.

2 Divide and stack the forty-two fat quarter strips into three piles of fourteen colors each.

3 Take one stack of strips from Step 2 and divide them in half so there are seven colors in each stack. All of the colors will be used, so it doesn't really matter which colors are in which stack. Stack neatly and place them on a cutting mat. Set aside the two remaining fourteen-piece stacks of strips.

NOTE: When you have used up the first two seven-piece stacks of strips, repeat Step 3 to divide up the second stack of fourteen strips, and then the third stack.

4 Begin with one Citrus Template A, and from one stack of seven strips, cut ten of Piece 1, following the size indicated on the pattern and cutting all seven fabrics at once. (Three colors will be cut twice.) Using the other stack of seven strips, cut ten of Piece 2, once again following the size indicated on the pattern and cutting all seven fabrics at once.

5 Refer to ***My Method: Paper Piecing*** (page 67) to sew down the pieces. Chain piecing (page 16) works really well here.

6 Cut pieces 3 and 4, making sure to switch out a few colors for a more random look. Sew down these pieces. Repeat this process to cut and sew all eight pieces for Template A. Make a total of ten half circles A.

7 Repeat steps 3 through 6 to make ten each of Template B, Template C, and Template D, for a total of forty half-circles.

8 Pair the A's with the B's, and the C's with the D's (although you can switch the letters around if you like). Remove the paper in the seams and sew together the half-circle pairs with right sides facing. Press the seams open and carefully remove all the paper.

If you're very organized, you can continue to cut and sew all the pieces for A, rotating the fabrics and mixing a few of them within the two stacks to create a more random look. If organization is not your strong point, cut and sew only two to four pieces at a time.

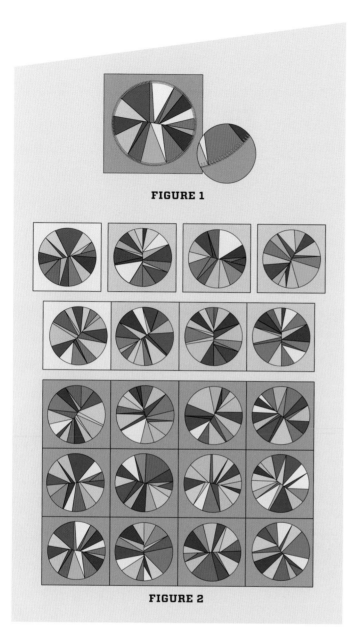

FIGURE 1

FIGURE 2

only. Turn the circle right side out and finger press the edges flat. Press around the edges with a hot iron until the circle is nice and flat, but don't leave the iron on your circle for too long. Repeat for all twenty circles.

3 To complete the block, center each circle on a square F of white, light gray, or dark gray background fabric 10½" × 10½" (26.5 × 26.5 cm). Use a clear acrylic ruler as a guide, if needed. Pin into place. Note that you will have an extra light gray square 10½" × 10½" (26.5 × 26.5 cm), which will be Piece G in the final quilt top.

4 Machine-appliqué each circle in place (*Fig. 1*). A blanket stitch looks really nice, but you could also use a zigzag stitch.

ASSEMBLE THE QUILT TOP
Press all seams open.

1 Refer to the **Citrus Assembly Diagram** to put together the quilt top. To complete the section of F blocks, sew together the 20 circle blocks into 5 rows of 5 blocks each. Refer to Figure 2 for the background color order.

2 As shown in the **Citrus Assembly Diagram**, sew Piece D to Piece E to complete the left side.

3 To assemble the right side, sew H to I, and J to K. Sew G to HI, then to JK, and then finally to Piece L.

4 For the top row, sew A to B, and then sew B to C. For the bottom row, sew M to N.

5 To complete the quilt top, sew the left, right, top, and bottom sections to Section F.

LINE AND APPLIQUÉ THE CIRCLES

1 To line the sewn circles, place one circle right side up on the stabilizer. Using a rotary cutter or very sharp fabric scissors, cut out twenty circles using a complete copy of the templates taped together.

2 Place one circle right side up and align a circle of stabilizer on top. Sew a ¼" (6 mm) seam all around the circle. Cut a 4"–5" (10–12.5 cm) opening through the stabilizer

> ### TIP
> If you need to add a white fabric lining to prevent the background from showing through, trace the circle onto the white fabric, and cut it out. Place the white circle right side up, then the colored circle right side up, and the stabilizer on top. Sew along the edge of the circle with a ¼" (6 mm) seam. Carefully cut a slit in the stabilizer only, and pull the circle right side out.

FINISH THE QUILT

1 Cut the backing fabric in half to make two pieces 42" × 90" (106.5 × 228.6 cm). Sew a ½" (1.3 cm) seam along the longest side of the two pieces with right sides together.

2 Use your favorite method to layer and baste your quilt top, batting, and backing. Quilt as desired. I chose to hand-quilt around each circle to add color, visual interest, and texture.

3 Sew the binding strips together end to end diagonally, and use your preferred method to bind the quilt.

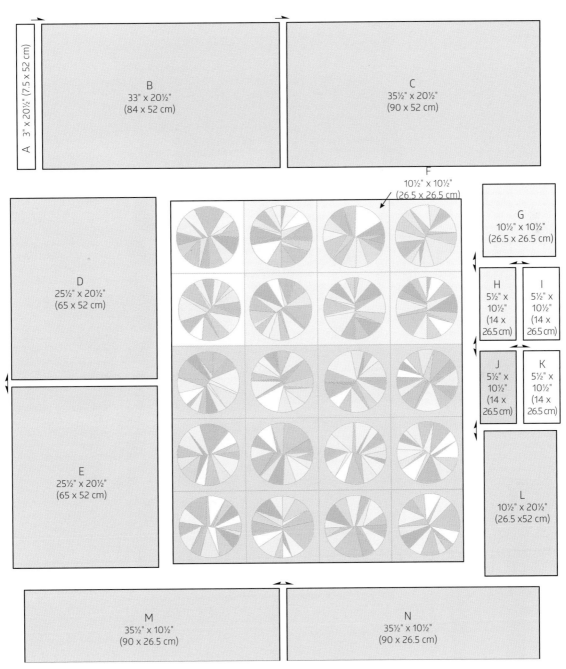

A 3" x 20½" (7.5 x 52 cm)

B
33" x 20½"
(84 x 52 cm)

C
35½" x 20½"
(90 x 52 cm)

D
25½" x 20½"
(65 x 52 cm)

E
25½" x 20½"
(65 x 52 cm)

F
10½" x 10½"
(26.5 x 26.5 cm)

G
10½" x 10½"
(26.5 x 26.5 cm)

H
5½" x 10½"
(14 x 26.5 cm)

I
5½" x 10½"
(14 x 26.5 cm)

J
5½" x 10½"
(14 x 26.5 cm)

K
5½" x 10½"
(14 x 26.5 cm)

L
10½" x 20½"
(26.5 x52 cm)

M
35½" x 10½"
(90 x 26.5 cm)

N
35½" x 10½"
(90 x 26.5 cm)

CITRUS ASSEMBLY DIAGRAM

MESA
quilt

#mesaquilt

My inspiration for this simple, high-impact design came from observing the dramatic mesas of the Southwest. I love the look of sharp angles against a neutral background. For the blue triangles, I used fabric from a thrift-shop janitor's shirt, and included its irregularities to offer visual interest. The negative space above the triangles welcomes design and quilting possibilities. This is a great gender-neutral quilt.

Finished Size:
57" × 70" (145 × 177.8 cm)

Materials
Yardage is based on fabric with a usable width of 42" (106.5 cm).

1 yd (91.5 cm) blue fabric

3½ yd (3.2 m) black fabric

4 yd (3.7 m) backing fabric

65" × 78" (165 × 199 cm) piece of batting

3" × 2½" (7.5 × 6.5 cm) colorful piece for contrast, optional

½ yd (45.5 cm) binding fabric

Cutting

WOF= width of fabric

Refer to the **Mesa Assembly Diagram** (page 81) to identify the lettered sections for the quilt top.

From blue fabric, cut:
3 strips 8¼" × WOF (21.5 cm × WOF); subcut into 26 pieces 3½" × 8¼" (9 × 21.5 cm) (A and C), and 7 squares 4¾" × 4¾" (12 × 12 cm) (B and D)

1 strip 4¾" × 23" (12 × 58.5 cm); subcut into 3 squares 4¾" × 4¾" (12 × 12 cm) (B and D), and 7 strips 1¼" × 3" (3.2 × 7.5 cm) (E).

From black fabric, cut:
2 strips 29" × WOF (73.5 cm × WOF). Subcut the first strip into 2 pieces 18" × 29" (45.5 × 73.5 cm) (K and L), and 2 strips 3" × 24¼" (7.5 × 61.5 cm) (I), and subcut the second strip into 2 pieces 18" × 29" (45.5 × 73.5 cm) (M and N), and 1 strip 5½" × 23" (14 × 58.5 cm) (H)

1 strip 5½" × WOF (14 cm × WOF); subcut into 1 strip 5½" × 35½" (14 × 90 cm) (J), 1 piece 2¼" × 3" (5.5 × 7.5 cm) (F), and 2 strips 1¼" × 3" (3.2 × 7.5 cm) (E)

1 strip 16" × WOF (40.5 cm × WOF); subcut into 2 strips 8" × 24¼" (20.5 × 61.5 cm) (O), 9 squares 4¾" × 4 ¾" (12 × 12 cm) (B and D), and 5 strips 1¼" × 3" (3.2 × 7.5 cm) (E)

2 strips 8¼" × WOF (21 cm × WOF); subcut into 24 strips 3½" × 8¼" (9 × 21 cm) (A and C)

1 strip 4¾" × WOF (12 cm × WOF); subcut into 2 strips 3½" × 8¼" (9 × 21 cm)(A),

1 square 4¾" × 4¾" (12 × 12 cm) (B), and 1 strip 3" × 12¾" strip (7.5 × 32 cm) (G).

From binding fabric, cut:
7 strips 2½" × WOF (6.5 cm × WOF).

MESA QUILT

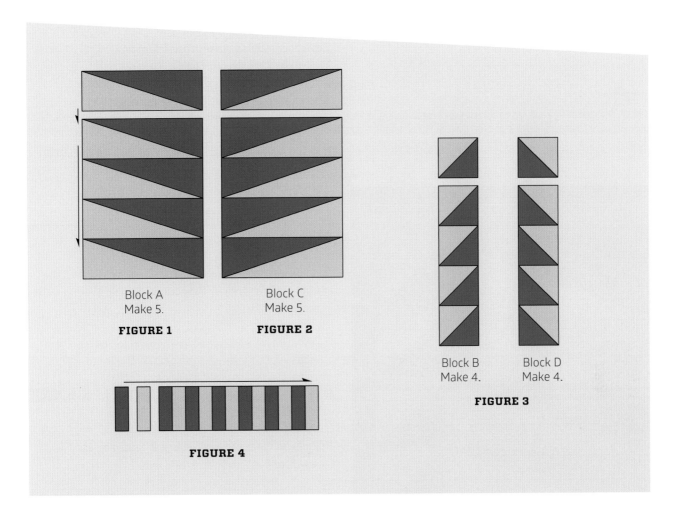

Block A
Make 5.

FIGURE 1

Block C
Make 5.

FIGURE 2

Block B
Make 4.

Block D
Make 4.

FIGURE 3

FIGURE 4

MAKE THE PIECED SECTIONS

Pieced sections A and C of this quilt are made with blue/black half-rectangle triangles (HRTs), and sections B and D are made using blue/black half-square triangles (HSTs). Press all seams open. Lock or backstitch at the start and end of stitching.

Sections A and C

1 Using thirteen black and thirteen blue A and C pieces 3½" × 8¼" (9 × 21.5 cm), refer to **My Method: Making Half-Rectangle Triangles** (page 82) to make twenty-six HRT units. Discard one unit. There are twenty-five units per section A and B. Trim to 3" × 8" (7.5 × 20.5 cm). Make five HRTs with the blue rectangles pointing right (**Fig. 1**). Make five sets.

2 Refer to the reverse HRT directions under **My Method: Making Half-Rectangle Triangles** (page 82) to make thirteen more HRTs using the remaining A and C

pieces 3½" × 8¼" (9 × 21.5 cm). Discard one unit. Trim to 3" × 8" (7.5 × 20.5 cm). Make five HRTs with the blue rectangles pointing left (**Fig. 2**). Make five sets.

Sections B and D

1 Refer to **My Method: Making Half-Square Triangles** (page 27) to make forty HSTs using the black and blue squares 4¾" × 4¾" (12 × 12 cm). Trim the squares to 3" × 3" (7.5 × 7.5 cm). For B, make five HSTs with the blue triangles in the upper left corner (**Fig. 3**). Make four sets. For D, make five HSTs with the blue triangles in the upper right corner (**Fig. 3**). Make four sets.

Section E

Piece together all fourteen black and blue strips 1¼" × 3" (3.2 × 7.5 cm), starting with the black and alternating the colors (**Fig. 4**).

MAKE THE QUILT TOP

*Refer to the **Mesa Assembly Diagram** to sew together the sections for the quilt top.*

1 Sew the A/B sections right sides together. Press the seams open. Make four sets.

2 Sew together all four sets, with the B sections on the right sides as shown. Sew one additional Section A to the end of the strip (**Fig. 5**).

3 Sew the C/D sections right sides together. Press seams open. Make four sets.

4 Sew together all four sets, with the D sections on the right sides as shown. Sew one additional Section C to the end of the strip.

5 Sew the two Sections I together end to end, and sew them between the A/B and C/D sections as shown.

6 For Pieces O, sew together. Sew Piece O to the bottom of Blocks C and D.

7 Sew F to the bottom of Section E, and sew G to E/F. Sew H to the top of the E/F/G unit.

8 Sew together K and L along the 18" side. Repeat for M and N. Sew K/L to M/N.

9 Sew J and H to either side of the A/B/C/D unit.

10 Sew K–N to the top of the unit made in Step 8.

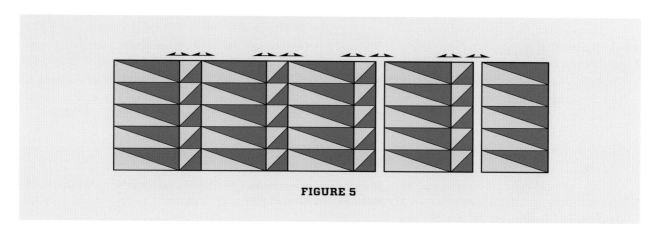

FIGURE 5

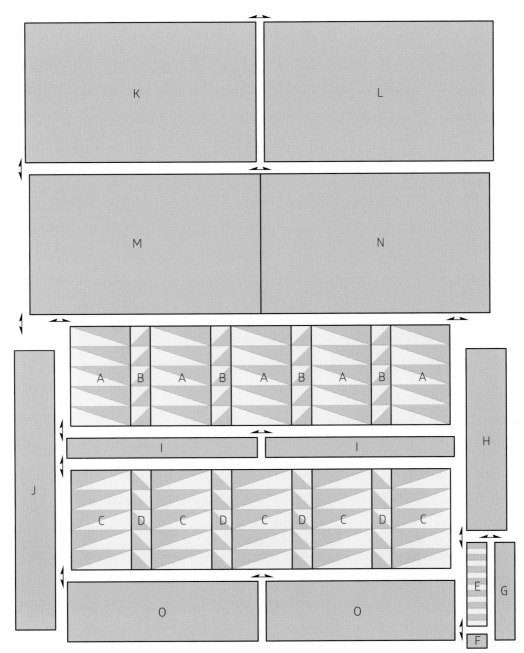

MESA ASSEMBLY DIAGRAM

FINISH THE QUILT

1 Cut the backing fabric in half and trim off the selvedges. Sew the two pieces together along the longest side using a ½" (1.3 cm) seam allowance. Press the seam open.

2 Use your favorite method to layer and baste your quilt top, batting, and backing. Quilt as desired. I heavily quilted the top, using a variety of free-motion motifs inside the triangles and simple channel quilting across the top of the quilt. But with all the available negative space in this design, you could take the opportunity to do special quilting in that area.

3 Sew the color accent binding piece 2½" × 3" (6.5 × 7.5 cm) to one end of your first black binding strip with right sides together, and sew along the edge. Press open. Sew the next black binding strip to the other end of the accent strip. Press open. Continue joining the binding strips end to end, and bind the quilt using your favorite method.

My Method: Making Half-Rectangle Triangles

This method creates two half-rectangle triangles at one time. Shown here are two versions: HRTs and reverse HRTs.

WHAT YOU'LL NEED

→ Fabric marking pen
→ Clear acrylic ruler
→ Rotary cutter and mat
→ Sewing pins

*Note: The diagonal line runs from upper left to lower right, no matter the orientation (**Fig. 1**). For reverse HRTs, see below.*

HERE'S HOW
HRTs

1 Cut the fabrics to the size specified in the project. Place your background fabric (Piece A) to the left with the right side facing up. Place your coordinating fabric (Piece B) to the right with the right side facing down (**Fig. 2**).

2 Draw an "A" that connects these two pieces. In the bottom left corner, mark a dot ½" (1.3 cm) in from the bottom and left side on piece A (**Fig. 3**). Mark another dot in the same manner but in the upper right corner on Piece A. Make the same marks on Piece B, but to continue that "A" shape, mark in the upper left and lower right side (**Fig 4**). Draw a line that connects the dots on both pieces.

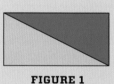

FIGURE 1

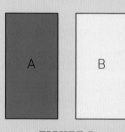

FIGURE 2

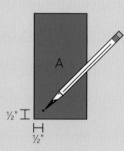

½" ⊥
⊢
½"

FIGURE 3

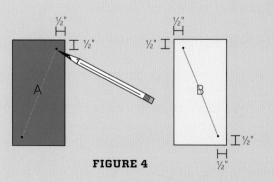

½"
½" ⊥

½"
½" ⊥

A

B

⊥ ½"
½"

FIGURE 4

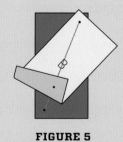

FIGURE 5

FIGURE 6

3 Pick up Piece B and slightly rotate it until the line you drew lines up with the line on Piece A. Pin into place (*Fig. 5*).

4 Sew a ¼" (6 mm) on either side using the line your marked as a guide (*Fig. 6*).

5 After sewing two lines, cut the along the marked line. Press the seams open (*Fig. 7*).

6 To trim your blocks, line up your ruler neatly with your unit. Place the ¼" (6 mm) marks on the diagonal line while maintaining the desired size you need (*Fig. 8*). It can be a little bit like a puzzle, so you may need to move your ruler around a little bit until you hit those marks. Trim away the excess. Rotate the unit, lining up the marks, and trim again.

For reversed HRTs

The diagonal line runs from lower left to upper right, no matter the orientation (*Fig. 9*).

Follow the steps for making HRTs. All the steps are the same with the exception of marking an "A." With your fabrics in the same position as noted in Step 1, draw a "V" instead of an "A" (*Fig 10*). Draw your line from the upper left corner dot to the bottom right corner on Piece A, and draw a line from bottom left corner to upper right corner on Piece B.

Continue with steps 4 to 6, as for HRTs.

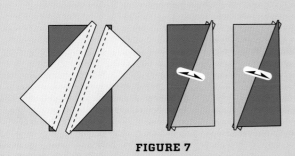

FIGURE 7

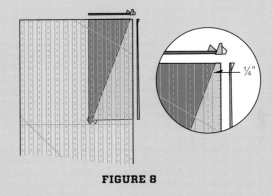

FIGURE 8

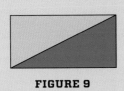

FIGURE 9

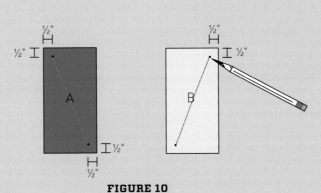

FIGURE 10

KALEIDOSCOPE
mini quilt

#kaleidoscopeminiquilt

Hexagons are a fun shape to sew, and in this design, I stitched individual flower-like "petals" with hexagons overlapping each other to create a kaleidoscope effect. Using the six basic colors of the color wheel, each in light, medium, and dark values, gives this quilt its special look; but do feel free to choose a different palette for a different effect. This design offers a lot of possibilities, and is a great scrap buster. The construction makes use of two different techniques: paper piecing and Y seams.

Finished Size:

18½" × 18½" (47 × 47 cm)

Materials

Yardage is based on fabric with a usable width of 42" (106.5 cm).

Scraps in light, medium, and dark values of 6 different colors.*

Scraps of cream fabric

½ yd (45.5 cm) background fabric

1 piece 26" × 26" (66 × 66 cm) backing fabric

1 piece 26" × 26" (66 × 66 cm) batting

1 fat quarter, 18" × 22" (45.5 × 56 cm) binding fabric**

* I used red, orange, yellow, green, blue, and violet.

**I used the same cream fabric as the one for the petals.

KALEIDOSCOPE MINI QUILT

Tools

Cardboard or heavy paper for Hexagon template patterns

Computer or copy paper for the Petal paper piecing templates

6 copies each of Kaleidoscope Petal Template Patterns A, B, C, and D (page 153)

1 copy of the Kaleidoscope Hexagon Template Pattern (page 152)

Cutting

From assorted scraps, cut:

108 pieces 3½" × 5½" (9 × 14 cm) pieces.*

From binding fabric, cut:
4 strips 2⅓" × 22" (6.5 × 56 cm).

* This piece size will be large enough for the largest paper piecing template areas; other areas will not require this much fabric.

> ### TIP
> When choosing your fabrics, try laying out various combinations. To achieve the effect in the original, use fabrics reflecting a rainbow.

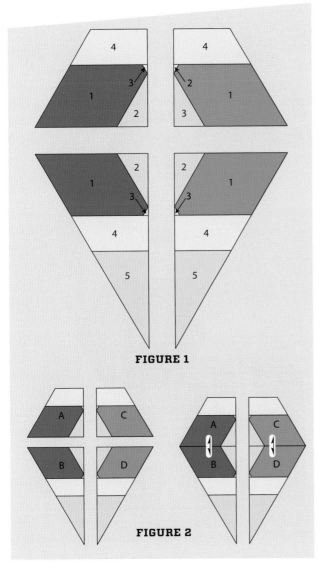

FIGURE 1

FIGURE 2

ASSEMBLE THE QUILT TOP

1 Refer to *My Method: Paper Piecing* (page 67) to make and cut out six each of Petal templates A, B, C, and D.

2 Make a sturdy cardboard template for the Hexagon template (see Spotlight, below). On the background fabric, trace around the template sixteen times; cut out sixteen hexagons and set them aside.

3 Sew down the assorted fabric pieces onto each of the Petal templates. Remember to sew on the pieces in numerical order (*Fig. 1*). The sewing order is switched for the top pieces on the pattern to help the points line up. For color placement, refer to the Kaleidoscope quilt illustration (facing page).

4 Sew together the pieced units for the petals. With right side sides together and making sure all seams line up (*Fig. 2*), pin or glue baste the units into place. Sew Piece A and B together, and sew C and D together to create two half-petals. Press the seams open. Repeat for the other petals.

5 Sew together the two half-petals. Press the seam open. Repeat to make six petals.

Spotlight

To cut out the multiple hexagons for this quilt, you will want to make the Hexagon Template on durable cardstock or cardboard rather than on regular paper, which can tear easily.

Copy and cut out your pattern, then trace it onto the cardboard. You can put tape on the back to keep it from moving around, and use a ruler for straight, accurate edges.

Carefully cut out the new cardboard template. Although you can use it multiple times, do check periodically to make sure that your template doesn't get trimmed off little by little during cutting.

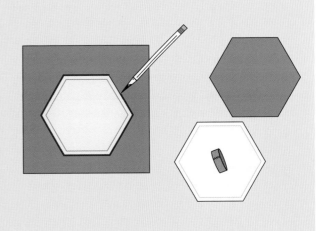

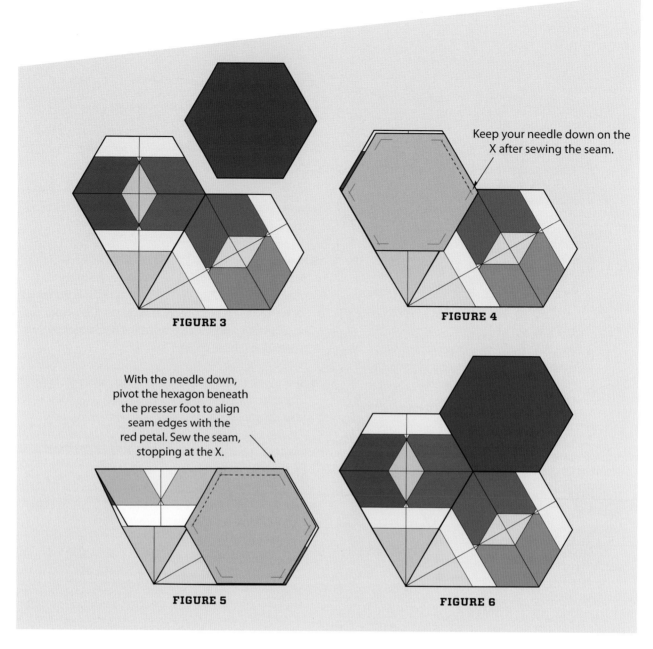

FIGURE 3

Keep your needle down on the X after sewing the seam.

FIGURE 4

With the needle down, pivot the hexagon beneath the presser foot to align seam edges with the red petal. Sew the seam, stopping at the X.

FIGURE 5

FIGURE 6

6 Now add the background hexagons. Starting ¼" (6 mm) from the top, sew two petals together and press the seams open (**Fig 3**). Backstitch at the beginning of sewing, so the seam will not come apart when inserting a hexagon later. Sew the petals together in two sets of three each. The ¼" (6 mm) gap is there so you can insert a hexagon between two petals to begin building the quilt background in the final assembly (Steps 7 and 8). Sew the two sets together. Press the seams open to help distribute the bulk in the center. You can also trim away the excess bulk, carefully avoiding snipping into any of the seams.

7 Following the instructions under **My Method: Sewing Y Seams** (page 90), sew a background hexagon between the red and orange petal units as shown (**Figs. 3, 4, 5, 6**). Press.

8 Continue sewing the remaining eleven hexagons clockwise around the center petal unit. To complete the quilt top, add an additional hexagon to each corner. Press.

KALEIDOSCOPE ASSEMBLY DIAGRAM

FINISH THE QUILT

1 Square up the quilt top by measuring 2" (5 cm) from the outer edges of the petals on each side. The trimmed top should measure 18½" × 18½" (47 × 47 cm).

2 Use your favorite method to layer and baste your quilt top, batting, and backing. Quilt as desired. I chose to echo-quilt within the petals to make the design pop a bit more than straight lines would have allowed.

3 Sew the binding strips together end to end diagonally, and use your preferred method to bind the quilt.

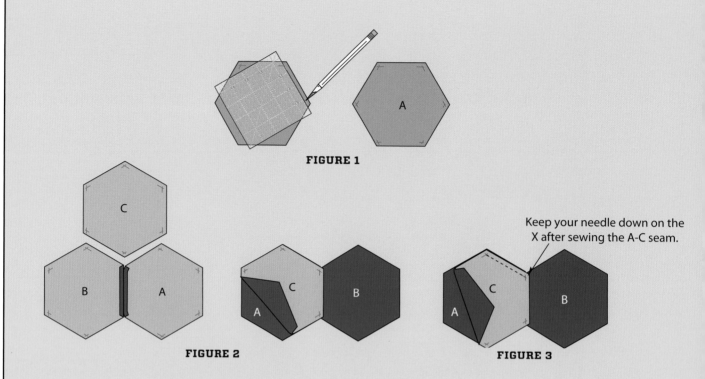

FIGURE 1

FIGURE 2

FIGURE 3

Keep your needle down on the X after sewing the A-C seam.

My Method: Sewing Y Seams

The technique for Y seams (sometimes called set-in seams) calls for sewing together three pieces of fabric so that three seams meet to form a "Y." It's often used to sew together hexagons or stars. The technique may seem complicated, but if you practice a few times to understand the way it works, the way the fabrics behave under the needle, and the mistakes to avoid, you'll sew through these in a breeze. Seriously.

The directions that follow refer to sewing together hexagons, like those used in the Kaleidoscope Quilt (page 84). But the same technique can be used anytime you want to join three fabrics together. If this is your first time sewing Y seams, I recommend cutting out four or five hexagons from scrap fabric and practicing on them before diving into your project.

WHAT YOU'LL NEED

→ Fabric marking pen
→ Small acrylic ruler
→ Tweezers
→ Fabric cut as indicated in the pattern you are using

HERE'S HOW

In this example, we're sewing together three hexagons—Hexagons A, B, and C.

1 All seams must start and stop ¼" (6 mm) from the edges of the hexagons. To make accurate sewing easier, place each hexagon wrong side up, measure ¼" (6 mm) in from each edge, and mark X's for the start and finish points (***Fig. 1***). (If you wish, you can keep a pen and small ruler near your sewing machine and add X marks as you sew.)

2 With right sides facing, sew together Hexagons A and B from X to X, using a ¼" (6 mm) seam. Make sure to backstitch at each start and stop point. Be careful to not go past your ¼" (6 mm) mark. Double check that there is a ¼" (6 mm) gap at the end of each seam (***Fig. 2***). Press the seam open. Now you're ready to insert Hexagon C using a Y seam. The X marks should be positioned as shown (***Fig. 2***). With right sides together, line up one side of C to one side of A.

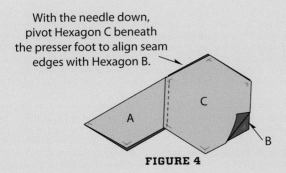

With the needle down, pivot Hexagon C beneath the presser foot to align seam edges with Hexagon B.

FIGURE 4

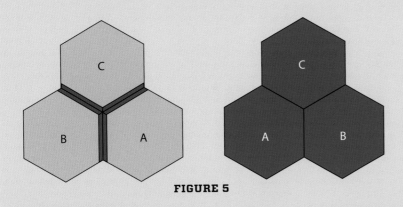

FIGURE 5

3 Beginning at the first X, sew a few stitches and then backstitch, making sure you don't go past the X and into the seam. Continue to sew a ¼" (6 mm) seam. When you get really close to the next X, go slowly, taking it one stitch at a time. You want your needle to land *exactly in the seam line* between A and B (*Fig. 3*). Leave your needle in the down position. Take a pair of tweezers, if needed, and lift up the top hexagon slightly until you can see the needle position. Sometimes I manually place my needle there or lower the stitch length to get it to land in the exact spot. Works like a charm every time!

4 Now pivot Hexagon C to the right, so it lines up with the edge of Hexagon B (*Fig. 4*). Then turn the entire piece to the left, so the edges run vertically with the sewing foot. In a perfect world, the pieces should naturally fall into place, and typically, they do. Sometimes there is a small bunch of fabric caught up around the needle. Use the tweezers to move the fabric into place, if necessary.

5 Make sure that Hexagon C lines up with the edge of Hexagon B and that they meet up exactly at the top edges. If so, you are good to sew to the next X. (If they don't, inaccurate seams or cutting may be the problem.) Sew to the next X, landing directly on the X and backstitching. Press the seams open (*Fig. 5*). You did it—you've sewn a Y seam!

TIP

The bias edges in the hexagons do stretch, and you can use this to your advantage by letting it help you position the hexagons correctly. But be careful to not stretch the fabric so much that it causes distortion. You don't want any folds or puckers in your seam line.

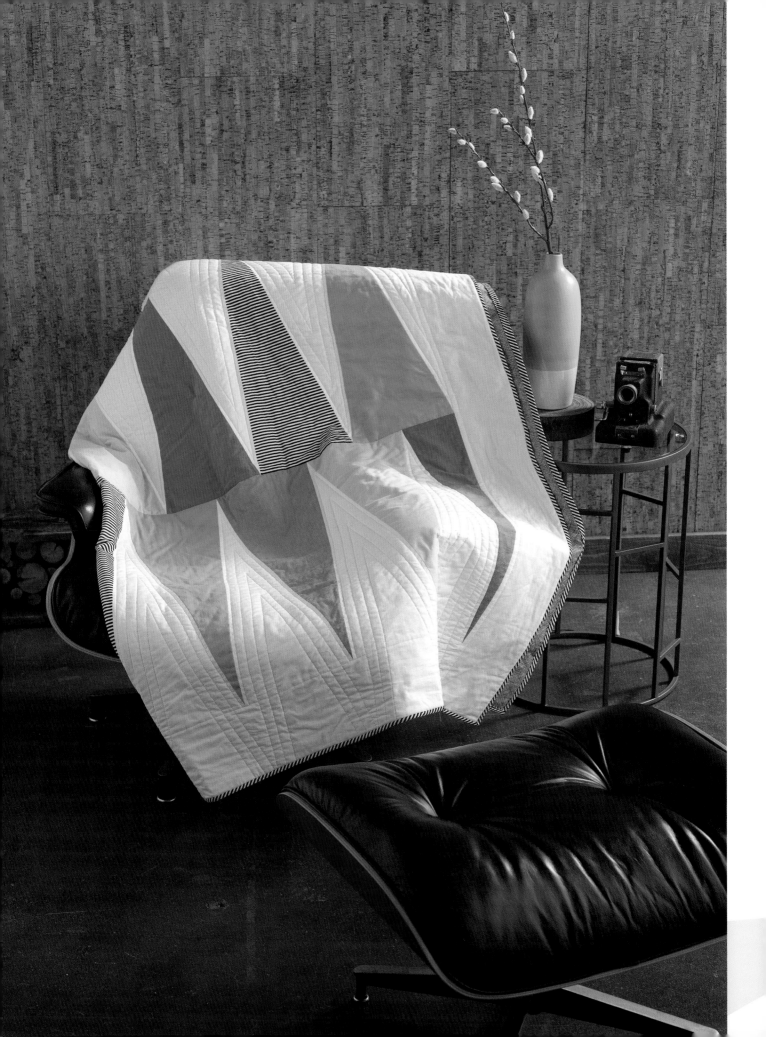

CIRCUS
quilt

#circusquilt

I love the cheerful colors in this quilt, and the triangle shapes look to me like flags flying on an old-time circus tent. The long, sharp angles are highlighted against a bright white background. To create these large triangles, you'll make your own template, which is easy to do. This bold, simple design has loads of impact and can be made in any colors you like.

Finished Size:
60" × 69" (125.5 × 175.25 cm)

Materials

Yardage is based on fabric with a usable width of 42" (106.5 cm).

1 yd (91.5 cm) each of red, green, striped, gray, and blue fabrics

3 yd (3.2 m) white fabric for the background and borders

5 yd (4.5 m) backing fabric

70" × 90" (178 × 229 cm) piece of batting

½ yd (45.5 cm) binding fabric

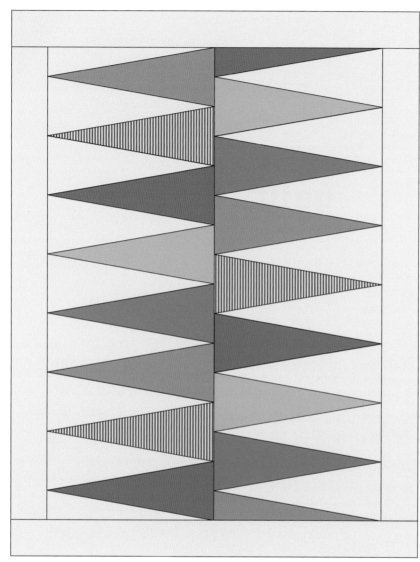

CIRCUS QUILT

Tools

Heavy paper or lightweight cardboard for template*

Flexible tape measure

Yardstick

Note: The triangle template measures about 9½" (24 cm) wide and 27" (68.5 cm) tall, so you'll need to make it from something more substantial than regular paper. Use the largest size of template material you can find, such as poster-size cardstock or cereal boxes. You may still have to tape pieces together to achieve the full size.

Cutting

WOF= width of fabric

From red fabric, cut:
1 piece 27" × 26" (68.5 × 66 cm).

From green fabric, cut:
1 piece 27" × 26" (68.5 × 66 cm).

From striped fabric, cut:
1 piece 27" × 22" (68.5 × 56 cm).

From gray fabric, cut:
1 piece 27" × 22" (68.5 × 56 cm).

From blue fabric, cut:
1 piece 27" × 22" (68.5 × 56 cm).

From white fabric, cut:
3 pieces 27" × WOF (68.5 cm × WOF) for the background

7 pieces 6" × WOF (15 cm × WOF) for the borders.

From binding fabric, cut:
7 strips 2½" × WOF (6.5 cm × WOF).

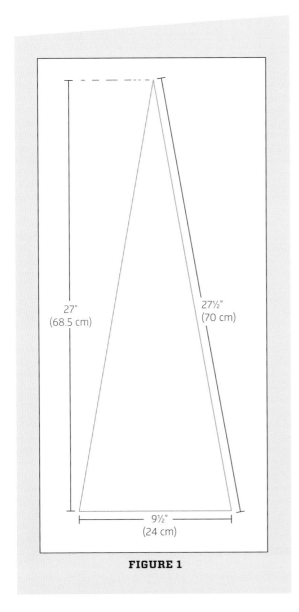

FIGURE 1

The template measurements shown: 27" (68.5 cm) height, 27½" (70 cm) angled side, 9½" (24 cm) wide.

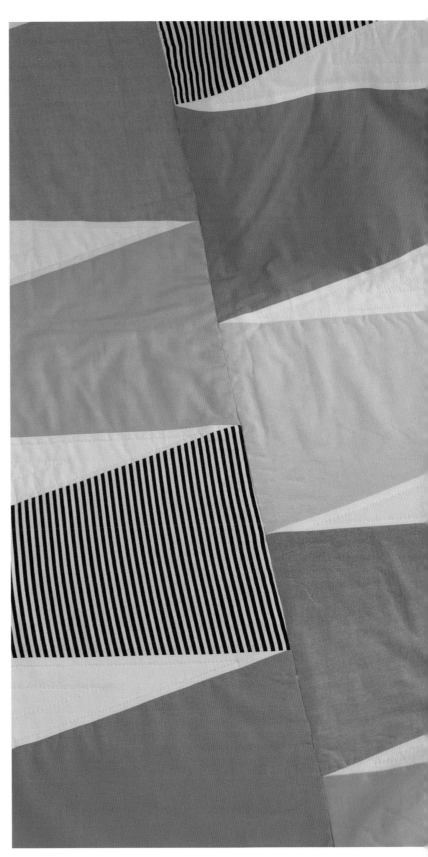

MAKE THE TEMPLATE

On the cardboard, use a long ruler or yardstick and a pencil to draw a triangle measuring 9½" (24 cm) wide and 27" (68.5 cm) high (**Fig. 1**). If your cardboard is not long enough, tape pieces together with sturdy tape until you can get the appropriate length. The angled sides should measure 27½" (70 cm).

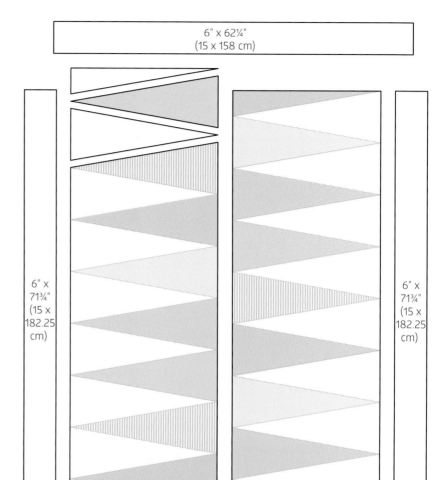

CIRCUS ASSEMBLY DIAGRAM

6" × 62¼"
(15 × 158 cm)

6" × 71¾" (15 × 182.25 cm)

6" × 71¾" (15 × 182.25 cm)

6" × 62¼"
(15 × 158 cm)

MAKE THE QUILT TOP

Seams are ¼" (6 mm) unless noted.

1 Using your template, cut out the triangles. Cut four triangles each from the red and green pieces. Cut three triangles each from the striped, gray, and blue pieces. Cut sixteen triangles from the white pieces 27" × WOF (68.5 cm × WOF). Cut one additional triangle from the remaining white fabric. Position and cut the triangles very carefully in order to get them all fitted onto the fabric.

2 The quilt top is constructed in two panels. Refer to the **Circus Assembly Diagram** to lay out the triangles, alternating between white and colored triangles.

3 On the right panel, take the red triangle at the very top and the green triangle at the very bottom. Fold them in half lengthwise and press. Open up each triangle, and using a long acrylic ruler, place the ¼" (6 mm) mark along the crease. With a washable fabric marker, mark along the edge of the ruler (***Fig. 2***).

4 Cut along the line. You won't need the smaller half of each triangle—you can save them in your scrap bin (***Fig. 3***).

5 Take the white triangles for the top and bottom of the left panel, and repeat steps 3 and 4.

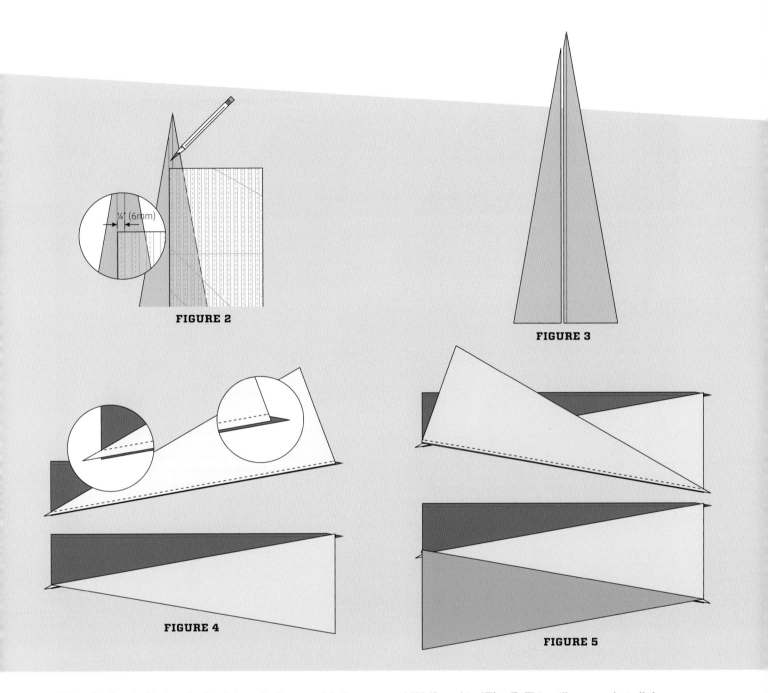

FIGURE 2

FIGURE 3

FIGURE 4

FIGURE 5

6 Put the four half-triangles back into the layout with the straight edges facing up for the ones on top, and facing down for the ones at the bottom. Sewing the first three triangles will be the trickiest. Starting on the right side panel, pick up the first two triangles—the red half-triangle and a white triangle. Flip the white triangle over. For these first two, line up the ends base-to-point, right sides together, so that when you place your needle at the edge, it will produce a ¼" (6 mm) seam (**Fig. 4**). Sew, and press the seam open.

7 For the third triangle and hereafter, line up the base of the triangle to be sewn to the base of the previous triangle you sewed, so that you start exactly at the edge

and ¼" (6 mm) in (**Fig. 5**). This will ensure that all the bases of the triangles are straight.

8 Continue to sew the triangles as in steps 6 and 7 to complete the right panel of the quilt top. Press toward the darker fabric.

9 Repeat steps 6 to 8 to complete the left panel. Trim off all the dog ears on both panels. Carefully snip off all of the excess triangle points on the back of the quilt to reduce the bulk in the seam allowance.

10 Sew together the two panels together using a ½" (1.3 cm) seam.

ADD THE BORDERS

Trim two of the border pieces 6" × WOF (15 cm × WOF) to 6" × 30¼" (15 cm × 76.8 cm). Sew each of these pieces to two full WOF border pieces to create two side borders 6" × 71¾" (15 × 182.5 cm) long. Sew these to the sides of the quilt top, using a ¼" (6 mm) seam. Next, cut one border piece 6" × WOF (15 cm × WOF) into two pieces 6" × 20¾" (15 cm × 52.7). Sew each piece to the last two border pieces to create two strips 6" × 62½" (15 cm × 158.75) long. These are your top and bottom borders; attach them using a ¼" (6 mm) seam. Carefully trim excess fabric.

FINISH THE QUILT

1 Trim the selvedges off the backing fabric, and cut two pieces 42" × 90" (106.5 × 229 cm). Sew them back together along the two longest sides, using a ½" (1.3 cm) seam. Press the seam open.

2 Use your favorite method to layer and baste your quilt top, batting, and backing. Quilt as desired. I used some very simple parallel lines on the background and left the triangles unquilted.

3 Sew the binding strips together end to end diagonally, and use your preferred method to bind the quilt.

> **TIP**
>
> These border pieces are long! To accurately sew them to the quilt, find the center of each long strip and of the main quilt body, and match them right sides together. Pin in place, working out from the center, and then stitch them in place, easing the fabric through gently so that you don't distort the top edges of the quilt. If your quilt body is square, this will keep the entire quilt square.

DESERT BLOOMS MEDALLION **quilt**

Medallion quilts typically have a central focal point, often surrounded by multiple borders. For this medallion quilt, I took a nontraditional route when planning colors and layout, taking my cues from the brilliant colors of desert flowers. As I progressed, I let each finished border suggest to me what colors to use in the next. Working with fabrics from a few collections helped make the colors cohesive. This flexible design allows you to easily add or subtract borders to make this quilt almost any size. As presented here, this is the perfect size for a baby or small lap quilt.

Finished Size:

52" × 52" (132 × 132 cm)

Materials

Yardage is based on fabric with a usable width of 42" (106.5 cm).

For Quilt Center:

⅜ yd (34.5 cm) navy geometric fabric

⅜ yd (34.5 cm) white fabric

2 strips 2½" × 4½" (6.5 × 11.5 cm) aqua fabric—these can be cut from a fat quarter or can be scraps from your stash

⅛ yd (11.5 cm) coral print fabric

¼ yd (23 cm) navy floral fabric

For Border 1:

½ yd (45.5 cm) yellow fabric

½ yd (45.5 cm) pink fabric

½ yd (45.5 cm) aqua fabric

Scraps of fabric for 4 cornerstones*

For Border 2:

⅜ yd (34.5 cm) white fabric (I used a print with white background)

Scraps of fabric for 4 cornerstones*

For Border 3:

Mixed scraps of various prints totaling ⅜ yd (34.5 cm) or ⅜ yd (34.5 cm) white fabric

½ yd (45.5 cm) navy fabric

Scraps of fabric for 4 cornerstones*

For Border 4:

⅜ yd (34.5 cm) white fabric

½ yd (45.5 cm) navy fabric

Scraps of fabric for 4 cornerstones*

For Border 5:

⅜ yd (34.5 cm) white fabric

⅜ yd (34.5 cm) pink fabric

Other materials:

2¾ yd (2.5 m) backing fabric

60" × 60" (152.5 × 152.5 cm) piece of batting

½ yd (45.5 cm) binding fabric

* When choosing scraps of various prints for the cornerstones, keep in mind that you will need enough to cut squares of the dimensions given in the Cutting list. For the cornerstones in each border, I fussy cut motifs from some favorite novelty fabrics.

Tools

Paper for paper piecing

Diamond Template Pattern (page 157)

TIP

When cutting skinny strips, it's sometimes easier to cut a wider WOF strip, then cut the lengths needed, then trim to the skinny strip required for the block assembly.

Cutting

WOF= width of fabric.

As you cut the pieces for each section, set each group aside in a separate pile with a label to identify them.

For quilt center:
From navy geometric fabric, cut:
2 strips 2½" × 8½" (6.5 × 21.5 cm)

4 strips 2½" × 4½" (6.5 × 11.5 cm)

2 strips 2½" × 4½" (6.5 × 11.5 cm) (for Flying Geese units)

4 squares 2½" × 2½" (6.5 × 11.5 cm) (for Flying Geese units).

From white fabric, cut:
8 squares 2½" × 2½" (6.5 × 11.5 cm)

2 strips 2½" × 4½" (6.5 × 11.5 cm)

4 squares 2½" × 2½" (6.5 × 6.5 cm) (for Flying Geese units)

1 strip 4½" × 22 ⅕"(11.5 × 57cm); subcut into 5 squares 4½" × 4½" (11.5 × 11.5 cm) (for HSTs).

From aqua fabric, cut:
2 strips 2½" × 4½" (6.5 × 11.5 cm).

From coral fabric, cut:
1 strip 4½" × 22⅕"(11.5 × 57 cm); subcut into 5 squares 4½" × 4½" (11.5 × 11.5 cm) (for HSTs).

From navy floral fabric, cut:
2 strips 2½" × WOF (6.5 cm × WOF); subcut into 4 strips 8½" × 2½" (21.5 × 6.5 cm), 4 strips 6½" × 2½" (16.5 × 6.5 cm), and 4 strips 4½" × 2½" (11.5 × 6.5 cm).

1 strip 2½" × 10" (6.5 × 25.5 cm); subcut into 4 squares 2½" × 2½" (6.5 × 6.5 cm).

For Border 1:
From yellow fabric, cut:
5 strips 3" × WOF (7.5 cm × WOF); subcut into 40 rectangles 3" × 5" (7.5 × 12.5 cm).

From pink fabric, cut:
6 strips 3" × WOF (7.5 cm × WOF); subcut into 80 strips 2" × 3" (5 × 7.5 cm).

From aqua fabric, cut:
6 strips 3" × WOF (7.5 cm × WOF); subcut into 80 strips 2" × 3" (5 × 7.5 cm).

From cornerstone fabric, cut:
4 squares 4½" × 4½" (11.5 × 11.5 cm).

For Border 2:
From white print fabric, cut:
4 strips 2½" × 28½" (6.5 × 72.5 cm).

From cornerstone fabric, cut:
4 squares 2½" × 2½" (6.5 × 6.5 cm).

For Border 3:
From various prints or white fabric, cut:
2 strips 5¼" × WOF (13.5 cm × WOF); subcut into 16 squares 5¼" × 5¼" (13.5 × 13.5 cm).

From navy fabric, cut:
5 strips 2⅞" × WOF (7.3 cm × WOF); subcut into 64 squares 2⅞" × 2⅞" (7.3 × 7.3 cm).

From cornerstone fabric, cut:
4 squares 4½" × 4½" (11.5 × 11.5 cm).

For Border 4:
From white fabric, cut:
1 strip 6" × WOF (15 cm × WOF); subcut into 16 strips 1½" × 10½" (3.8 × 26.5 cm).

1 strip 4½" × WOF (11.5 cm × WOF); subcut into 16 strips 1½" × 6½" (3.8 × 16.5 cm).

1 strip 1 ½" × WOF (3.8 cm × WOF); subcut into 16 strips 1½" × 2½" (3.8 × 6.5 cm).

From navy fabric, cut:
1 strip 6" × WOF (15 cm × WOF); subcut into 16 strips 1½" × 10½" (3.8 × 26.5 cm) .

1 strip 9" × WOF (23 cm × WOF); subcut into 6 strips 1½" × WOF (3.8 cm × WOF); subcut into 32 strips 4½" × 1½" (11.5 × 3.8 cm) and 32 strips 2½" × 1½" (6.5 × 3.8 cm).

From cornerstone fabric, cut:
4 squares 4½" × 4½" (11.5 × 11.5 cm).

For Border 5:
From white fabric, cut:
3 strips 4½" × WOF (11.5 cm × WOF) strips; subcut into 25 squares 4½" × 4½" (11.5 × 11.5 cm).

From pink fabric, cut:
3 strips 4½" × WOF (11.5 cm × WOF) strips; subcut into 25 squares 4½" × 4½" (11.5 × 11.5 cm).

For binding:
From binding fabric, cut:
6 strips 2½" × WOF (6.5 cm × WOF).

DESERT BLOOMS MEDALLION QUILT

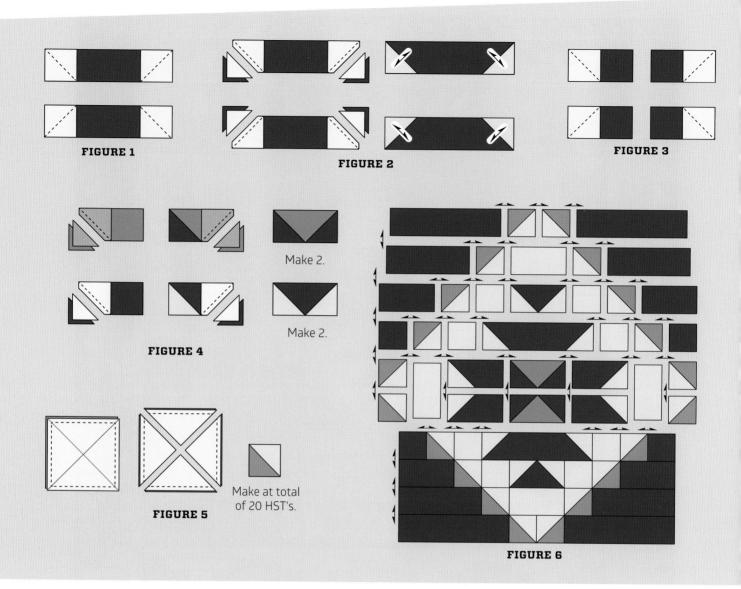

FIGURE 1

FIGURE 2

FIGURE 3

FIGURE 4

Make 2.

Make 2.

FIGURE 5

Make at total
of 20 HST's.

FIGURE 6

MAKE THE QUILT CENTER

The finished center measures 10½" × 10½" (26.5 × 26.5 cm). Press all seams open unless otherwise noted.

1 Lay the two navy geometric fabric strips 2½" × 8½" (6.5 × 21.5 cm) right sides up (**Fig. 1**). Place a white square 2½" × 2½" (6.5 × 6.5 cm) right side down on either end of each strip; pin in place. Mark a diagonal line on each white square as each as shown. Sew along the line, and trim the seam allowance to ¼" (6mm) (**Fig. 2**). Press open or to the side. Repeat for all both strips.

2 Lay the four navy geometric strips 2½" × 4½" (6.5 × 11.5 cm) right sides up (**Fig. 3**). Place a white square 2½" × 2½" (6.5 × 6.5 cm) right side down on one end of each strip. Mark, sew, trim, and press as for the strips in Step 1.

3 Refer to **My Method: Making Flying Geese** (page 110) to make two Flying Geese units using two aqua strips 2½" × 4½" (6.5 × 11.5 cm) and four navy geometric squares 2½" × 2½" (6.5 × 6.5 cm). Make two units using the two navy geometric strips 2½" × 4½" (6.5 × 11.5 cm) and the four white squares 2½" × 2½" (6.5 × 6.5 cm) (**Fig. 4**).

DESERT BLOOMS MEDALLION ASSEMBLY DIAGRAM

4 Refer to ***My Method: Making Half-Square Tri-angles*** (page 27), and use the Four units at a time method, with the white and coral print squares 4½" × 4½" (11.5 × 11.5 cm) (***Fig. 5***). Trim the finished HSTs to 2½" × 2½" (6.5 × 6.5 cm).

5 Lay out all the pieces for the quilt center as shown (***Fig. 6***), including the units made in steps 1 through 4, the white strips 2½" × 4½" (6.5 × 11.5 cm) and

remaining white squares, and all the navy floral pieces. Sew together the two middle rows. Then starting with the top row and going from left to right, sew together all the pieces for that row. Press the seams open. Sew together the pieces for each row and press.

6 Sew all the rows together, and press the seams open to complete the quilt center.

MAKE BORDER 1

1 Refer to **My Method: Paper Piecing** (page 67) to make and cut out forty Diamond templates.

2 Sew down the yellow, pink, and aqua pieces in numerical order, and make a total of forty diamond blocks.

3 With right sides together, sew together ten diamond blocks along the long edges to create one strip. Repeat to make a total of four strips. Press.

4 On one strip, sew a cornerstone 4½" × 4½" (11.5 × 11.5 cm) to each end (**Fig. 7**). Repeat with one more strip. Press the seams to the side.

5 Sew the two strips without cornerstones to the top and bottom of the quilt center (**Fig. 8**). Then sew the two strips with cornerstones to the sides to complete Border 1. Press the seams to the side.

MAKE BORDER 2

1 Sew a cornerstone 2½" × 2½" (6.5 × 6.5 cm) to each end of two of the white print strips 2½" × 28½" (6.5 × 72.5 cm).

2 Refer to the **Desert Blooms Medallion Assembly Diagram** (page 105) to sew the two white print strips without cornerstones to the top and bottom of Border 1. Press seams to the side.

3 Sew the two strips with cornerstones to the sides to complete Border 2. Press the seams to the side.

MAKE BORDER 3

1 Refer to **My Method: Making Flying Geese** (page 110) and use the Four units at a time instructions with the varied 5¼" × 5¼" (13.5 × 13.5 cm) squares and the navy squares 2⅞" × 2⅞" (7.3 × 7.3 cm) to make 64 Flying Geese units. Trim each to 2½" × 4½" (6.5 × 11.5 cm).

2 Sew together eight units with their points facing in the same direction (**Fig. 9**). Make a total of eight strips. Note: When you sew them to the quilt top, four of these strips will rotate 180 degrees.

3 Sew together two strips with the points facing towards each other as shown (**Fig. 10**). Make four strips.

4 Sew a cornerstone 4½" × 4½" (11.5 × 11.5 cm) to each end of two of the strips.

5 Sew the two strips without cornerstones to the top and bottom of Border 2. Press the seams to the side.

6 Sew the two strips with cornerstones to the sides to complete Border 3. Press the seams to the side.

MAKE BORDER 4

This border contains sixteen blocks.

1 To make one block, lay out the following as shown (**Fig. 11**):

→ 1 navy strip 1½" × 10½" (3.8 × 26.5 cm);

→ 2 navy strips 1½" × 6½" (3.8 × 16.5 cm) and 1 white strip 1½" × 2½" (3.8 × 6.5 cm);

→ 2 navy strips 1½" × 2½" (3.8 × 6.5 cm) and 1 white strip 1½" × 6½" (3.8 × 16.5 cm);

→ 1 white strip 1½" × 10½" (3.8 × 26.5 cm).

2 Sew the pieces together into block rows, press, and sew the rows together to create a block (**Fig. 12**), then press. Repeat to make a total of sixteen blocks. Trim each block to 10½" × 4½" (26.5 × 11.5 cm), centering the smallest middle rectangle in Row 2.

3 Sew four blocks together to create one long strip. Repeat to make four strips.

4 Sew a cornerstone 4½" × 4½" (11.5 × 11.5 cm) to each end of two of the border strips.

5 Sew the two strips without cornerstones to the top and bottom of Border 3. Press seams to the side.

6 Sew the two strips with cornerstones to the sides to complete Border 4. Press the seams to the side.

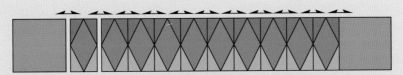

FIGURE 7

FIGURE 8

FIGURE 9

FIGURE 10

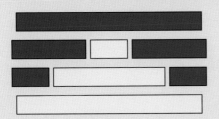

FIGURE 11

FIGURE 12

MAKE BORDER 5

1 Refer to ***My Method: Making Half-Square Triangles*** (page 27), and use the Four units at a time instructions with the white and pink squares 4½" × 4½" (11.5 × 11.5 cm) to make a total of 100 HSTs. Trim the finished units to 2¼" × 2¼" (5.5 cm × 5.5 cm).

2 Sew together thirteen HSTs into a strip with the diagonals going from upper left to lower right as shown (***Fig. 13***). Make two strips total. Sew together twelve HSTs oriented the same way; make two strips total. Press.

3 Sew together thirteen HSTs into a strip with the diagonals going the opposite direction, from bottom left to upper right (***Fig. 14***). Make two strips total. Sew twelve HSTs also oriented from bottom left to upper right; make two strips total. Press.

4 Sew together two opposing thirteen-piece strips as shown (***Fig. 15***). Make two long strips total. Sew the two opposing twelve-piece strips together; press.

5 Refer to the ***Desert Blooms Medallion Assembly Diagram*** (page 105) to sew the two shorter strips to the quilt top and bottom. Sew the two longer strips to either side. Press. This completes the quilt top.

FINISH THE QUILT

1 From the backing fabric, cut one strip 60" × WOF (152.5 cm × WOF). From the remainder of fabric, cut two strips 19" × WOF (48.5 cm × WOF).

2 Sew together the two strips along the 19" (48.5 cm) sides using a ½" (1.3 cm) seam allowance. Press the seam open. Sew this strip to the large piece of backing along the 60" (152.5 cm) side. Press open.

3 Use your favorite method to layer and baste your quilt top, batting, and backing. Quilt as desired. I used simple straight lines that would not distract from the array of prints in the design.

4 Sew together the binding strips end to end diagonally, and use your preferred method to bind the quilt.

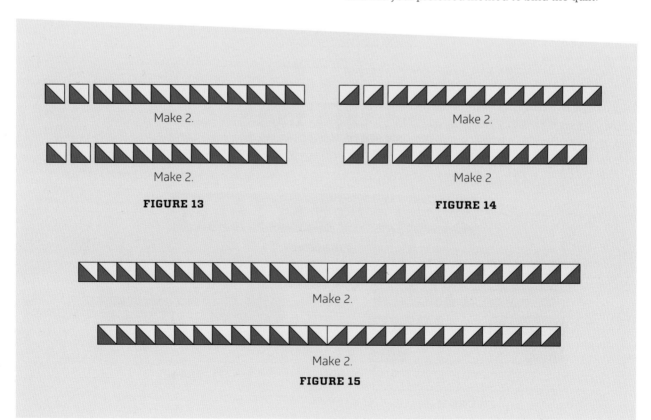

Make 2.

Make 2.

FIGURE 13

Make 2.

Make 2

FIGURE 14

Make 2.

Make 2.

FIGURE 15

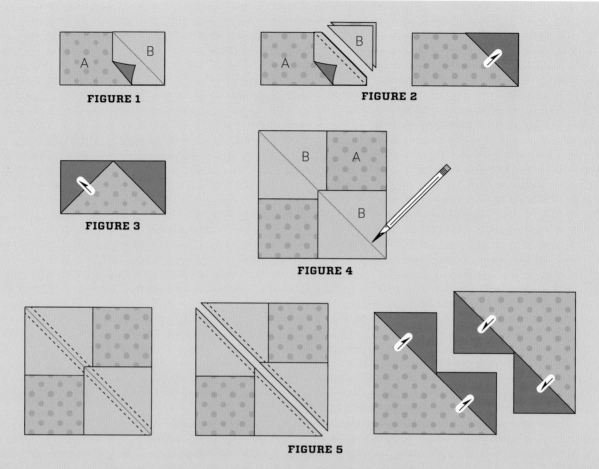

FIGURE 1

FIGURE 2

FIGURE 3

FIGURE 4

FIGURE 5

My Method: Making Flying Geese

You can make these simple, basic units either one at a time, or two at a time. Here are both methods.

WHAT YOU'LL NEED

→ Fabric marking pen
→ Clear acrylic ruler
→ Rotary cutter and mat
→ Flying Goose fabric, cut as indicated in the pattern you are using
→ Background fabric, cut as indicated in the pattern you are using

HERE'S HOW
One unit at a time

1 Cut out rectangles and squares from two contrasting or coordinating fabrics as indicated in the pattern you're using. Here we'll call the light fabric A and the darker fabric B.

2 Lay one rectangle A right side up, and place one square B right side down on the right-hand side. Using a ruler, mark a diagonal line from one corner to the other as shown (***Fig. 1***). Pin if desired.

3 Stitch along the marked line and trim, leaving a ¼" (6mm) seam allowance. Press the seam open or to the dark side (***Fig. 2***).

4 Repeat steps 2 and 3 for the left side of the rectangle A to yield one Flying Geese unit (***Fig. 3***).

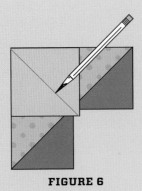

FIGURE 6

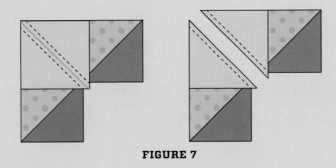

FIGURE 7

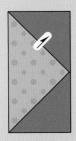

FIGURE 8

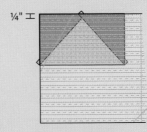

¼" ⊥

FIGURE 9

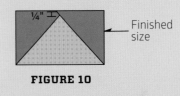

¼" ⊥

Finished size

FIGURE 10

Four units at a time

1 Cut out pieces from two contrasting or coordinating fabrics as indicated in the pattern you're using. Here, we'll call the large square of light fabric A and the darker fabric B.

2 Lay piece A right side up and place two squares B right side down, in opposite corners. Pin. Using a ruler, mark a diagonal line from one corner to the other as shown (*Fig. 4*).

3 Sew ¼" (6mm) on either side of the marked line and cut apart along the line (*Fig. 5*). Press the seam open or to the dark side on both units.

4 Place one unit right side up, and place another square B right side down in the corner, as shown (*Fig. 6*). Mark the square with a diagonal line corner to corner. Pin.

5 Sew ¼" (6mm) on either side of the marked line, and cut apart along the line (*Fig. 7*). Press the seam open or to the dark side on both units. This will yield two Flying Geese units (*Fig. 8*).

6 Repeat steps 4 and 5 for the remaining unit to yield four Flying Geese units.

HOW TO TRIM UNITS

Squaring up the Flying Geese units is important, so don't skip this step!

1 Place an acrylic ruler over the unit, lining it up near your desired measurements. In this example, the finished unit will be 2 ½" × 4 ½" (6.5 × 11.5 cm). Make sure that the tip of the triangle is ¼" away from the edge as shown (*Fig. 9*). This leaves you a seam allowance to avoid cutting off the tip when you stitch it to an adjoining piece of fabric. The tips at the base of the triangle will touch the 2 ½" (6.5 cm) and 4 ½" (11.5 cm) marks.

2 Trim the unit top and side. Then rotate the unit 180 degrees, lining it up perfectly with the ruler marks for your desired finished size, and trim the remaining two sides (*Fig. 10*).

FOUR CORNERS
quilt

#fourcornersquilt

When my husband and I drove across the country, we were awed by the beauty of the Southwest, especially in the areas surrounding the Four Corners Monument, where Colorado, New Mexico, Arizona, and Utah meet. I wanted to use the colors of the desert and combine them with graphic designs found in Turkish Kilim rugs. With the clever use of the half-square triangle, the resulting bold design is great for confident beginners.

Finished Size:

65½" × 75½" (166.4 × 191.8 cm)

Materials

Yardage is based on fabric with a usable width of 42" (106.5 cm).

1¼ yd (1.2 m) white solid fabric

1¼ yd (1.2 m) light blue solid fabric

1¼ yd (1.2 m) dark blue solid fabric

1¼ yd (1.2 m) orange solid fabric

1¼ yd (1.2 m) dark gray solid fabric

1¼ yd (1.2 m) pink solid fabric

4¼ yd (3.9 m) backing fabric

72" × 82" (182 × 209 cm) piece of batting

½ yd (45.5 cm) binding fabric

FOUR CORNERS QUILT

Tools

Small acrylic ruler with visible 45-degree angle, at least 3" (7.5 cm) square, or the Quilt in a Day Square Up Ruler*

A colored copy of the pattern to keep by your machine for visual guidance, optional

*See Option: Using a Special Ruler (page 29), under **My Method: Making Half-Square Triangles** (page 27).*

Cutting

WOF = width of fabric. HSTs = half square triangles

From each of the white and orange fabrics, cut:

6 strips 3" × WOF (7.5 cm × WOF); subcut into 72 squares 3" × 3" (7.5 × 7.5 cm) (for plain square units)

5 strips 5" × WOF (12.5 cm × WOF); subcut into 36 squares 5" × 5" (12.5 × 12.5 cm) (for HSTs).

From each of the light blue, dark blue, pink, and dark gray fabrics, cut:

5 strips 3" × WOF (7.5 cm × WOF); subcut into 60 squares 3" × 3" (7.5 × 7.5 cm) (for plain square units)

4 strips 5" × WOF (12.5 cm × WOF); subcut into 33 squares 5" × 5" (12.5 × 12.5 cm) (for HSTs).

From binding fabric, cut:
7 strips 2½" × WOF (6.5 cm × WOF).

> **TIP**
>
> I stacked my strips before subcutting them to save time and work. If you want to do it this way, make sure your rotary cutter has a sharp new blade.

MAKE THE HALF -SQUARE TRIANGLES

1. Place the 5" × 5" (12.5 × 12.5 cm) squares right sides together in pairs, in the following color combinations:

→ 18 pairs dark blue/white
→ 18 pairs white/orange
→ 18 pairs light blue/orange
→ 15 pairs light blue/dark gray
→ 15 pairs dark gray/pink
→ 15 pairs pink/dark blue

2 Refer to *My Method: Making Half-Square Triangles* (page 27), and use the Four units at a time method to make HSTs from the paired squares. Trim all the units to 3" × 3" (7.5 × 7.5 cm). You will have a total of seventy-two dark blue/white, seventy-two orange/white, seventy-two orange/light blue, sixty dark gray/light blue, sixty dark gray/pink, and sixty dark blue/pink HSTs.

TIP

Chain piecing helps make shorter work of sewing together the blocks. Refer to Chain Piecing (page 16) for information. Be consistent in the way you stack and place your pairs. You want to be able to pick up the pairs and feed them quickly through your sewing machine one after the other to speed up the process.

MAKE THE BLOCKS

This quilt is made using two blocks, A and B. Each block has five rows of thirteen HST units and plain squares 3" × 3" (7.5 × 7.5 cm). Each block is used six times in the quilt top.

The colors in Block A are arranged in diagonals from lower right to upper left, and all the HSTs slant from left to right. The colors in Block B are arranged in diagonals from lower left to upper right, and the all HSTs slant from right to left. Look at the **Four Corners Assembly Diagram** (page 119) to see how the blocks appear when arranged in the quilt top.

To keep the assembly process orderly, I recommend making all the A blocks before going on to the B blocks. When creating your blocks, make sure to lay them out before attempting to sew them together.

Block A

Because there are so many pieces in this quilt, you will find it easiest to assemble and sew the Row 1's for all the A blocks first, then move on to sew all the Row 2's, and so on (instead of sewing all six rows for one block and then repeating that five more times).

Stack the following combinations with right sides together. The HST diagonals will slant from upper left to lower right (**Fig. 1**). Be sure to orient each HST with the colors as shown in the diagram.

Row 1 (6 sets)

→ 6 dark blue/white HSTs and 6 white squares
→ 6 orange/white HSTs and 6 orange squares
→ 6 orange/light blue HSTs and 6 light blue squares
→ 6 light blue/dark gray HSTs and 6 dark gray squares
→ 6 dark gray/pink HSTs and 6 pink squares
→ 6 pink/dark blue HSTs and 6 dark blue squares
→ 6 dark blue/white HSTs

Row 2 (6 sets)

→ 6 white squares and 6 orange/white HSTs
→ 6 orange squares and 6 orange/light blue HSTs
→ 6 light blue squares and 6 light blue/dark gray HSTs
→ 6 dark gray squares and 6 dark gray/pink HSTs
→ 6 pink squares and 6 pink/dark blue HSTs
→ 6 dark blue squares and 6 dark blue/white HSTs
→ 6 white squares

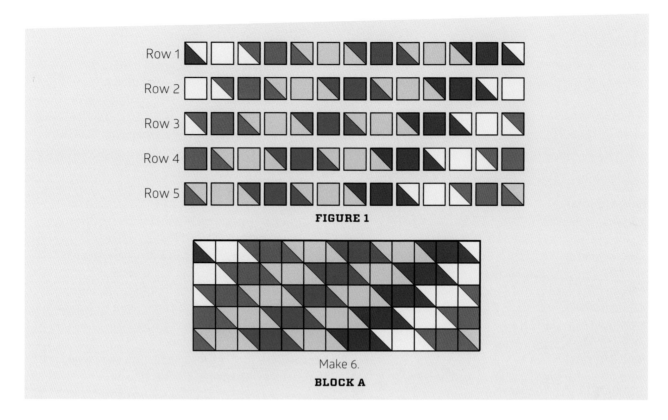

Row 1

Row 2

Row 3

Row 4

Row 5

FIGURE 1

Make 6.

BLOCK A

Row 3 (6 sets)

→ 6 white/orange HSTs and 6 orange squares
→ 6 orange/light blue HSTs and 6 light blue squares
→ 6 light blue/dark gray HSTs and 6 dark gray squares
→ 6 dark gray/pink HSTS and 6 pink squares
→ 6 pink/dark blue HSTs and 6 dark blue squares
→ 6 dark blue/white HSTs and 6 white squares
→ 6 white/orange HSTs

Row 4 (6 sets)

→ 6 orange squares and 6 orange/light blue HSTs
→ 6 light blue squares and 6 light blue/dark gray HSTs
→ 6 dark gray squares and 6 dark gray/pink HSTS
→ 6 pink squares and 6 pink/dark blue HSTs
→ 6 dark blue squares and 6 dark blue/white HSTs
→ 6 white squares and 6 white/orange HSTs
→ 6 orange squares

Row 5 (6 sets)

→ 6 orange/light blue HSTs and 6 light blue squares
→ 6 light blue/dark gray HSTs and 6 dark gray squares
→ 6 dark gray/pink HSTS and 6 pink squares
→ 6 pink/dark blue HSTs and 6 dark blue squares
→ 6 dark blue/white HSTs and 6 white squares
→ 6 white/orange HSTs and 6 orange squares
→ 6 orange/light blue HSTs

1 Chain piece all the combinations for Row 1 in their respective order to end up with six sets of Row 1. Clip the threads, and press the seams open.

2 Arrange the pairs back in the correct order, and sew the pairs together in their respective order. Lastly, sew six dark blue and white HSTs to the end of the blue squares when all the strips have been sewn. Make six Row 1 strips. Press the seams open. Set aside.

3 Repeat Steps 1 and 2 for Rows 2 to 5 for Block A. Units with no pair listed are sewn at the end of each row.

4 With right sides together and lining up the seams, pin or glue baste, then sew Rows 1 and 2 together. Repeat for Rows 3 and 4.

5 Sew the two sets together, followed by sewing Row 5 at the end to make Block A. Press the seams open.

Block B

As for Block A, assemble and sew the Row 1's for all the B blocks first, then move on to sew all the Row 2's, and so on.

Stack the following combinations with right sides together. The HST diagonals will slant from upper right to lower left (**Fig. 2**). Be sure to orient each HST with the colors as shown in the diagram.

Row 1 (6 sets)
→ 6 white/dark blue HSTs and 6 dark blue squares
→ 6 dark blue/pink HSTs and 6 pink squares
→ 6 pink/dark gray HSTs and 6 dark gray squares
→ 6 dark gray/light blue HSTs and 6 light blue squares
→ 6 light blue/orange HSTs and 6 orange squares
→ 6 orange/white HSTs and 6 white squares
→ 6 white/dark blue HSTs

Row 2 (6 sets)
→ 6 white squares and 6 white/dark blue HSTs
→ 6 dark blue squares ad 6 dark blue/pink HSTs
→ 6 pink squares and 6 pink/dark gray HSTs
→ 6 dark gray squares and 6 dark gray/light blue HSTs
→ 6 light blue squares and 6 light blue/orange HSTs
→ 6 orange squares and 6 orange/white HSTs
→ 6 white squares

Row 3 (6 sets)
→ 6 orange/white HSTs and 6 white squares
→ 6 white/dark blue HSTs and 6 dark blue squares
→ 6 dark blue/pink HSTs and 6 pink squares
→ 6 pink/dark gray HSTs and 6 dark gray squares
→ 6 dark gray/light blue HSTs and 6 light blue squares
→ 6 light blue/orange HSTs and 6 orange squares
→ 6 orange/white HSTs

Row 4 (6 sets)
→ 6 orange squares and 6 orange/white HSTs
→ 6 white squares and 6 white/dark blue HSTs
→ 6 dark blue squares and 6 dark blue/pink HSTs
→ 6 pink squares and 6 pink/dark gray HSTs
→ 6 dark gray squares and 6 dark gray/light blue HSTs
→ 6 light blue squares and 6 light blue/orange HSTs
→ 6 orange squares

Row 5 (6 sets)
→ 6 light blue/orange HSTs and 6 orange squares
→ 6 orange/white HSTs and 6 white squares
→ 6 white/dark blue HSTs and 6 dark blue squares
→ 6 dark blue/pink HSTs and 6 pink squares
→ 6 pink/dark gray HSTs and 6 dark gray squares
→ 6 dark gray/light blue HSTs and 6 light blue squares
→ 6 light blue/orange HSTs

Repeat Steps 1 to 5 for making Block A and sewing on the last unit with no pair, according to its respective row.

ASSEMBLE THE QUILT TOP

There are six quilt rows, each containing one A block and one B block.

1 Once all the blocks have been made, lay them out according to the **Four Corners Assembly Diagram**. The blocks in every other row must be rotated 180 degrees, reversing their direction to create the center pattern in each pair of quilt rows.

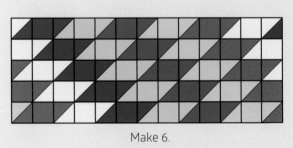

Make 6.

BLOCK B

Row 1
Row 2
Row 3
Row 4
Row 5

FIGURE 2

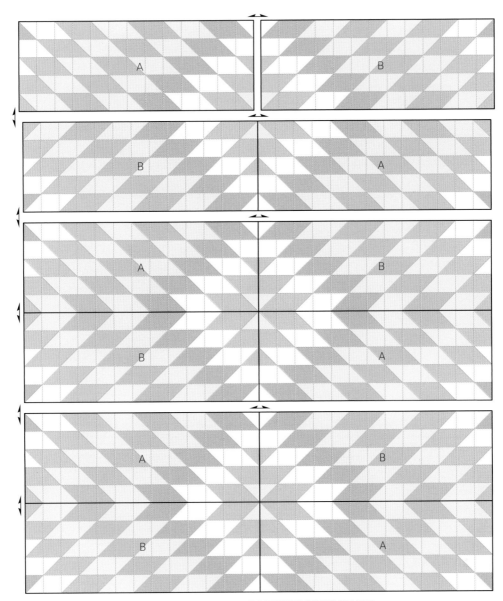

FOUR CORNERS ASSEMBLY DIAGRAM

2 For the top quilt row, align the seams, then pin or glue baste Block A to Block B right sides together, along the center edges. Sew, and press the seams open. Repeat to make three sets (quilt rows 1, 3, and 5).

3 For the second quilt row, rotate Block B and Block A and align the seams. Pin or glue baste Block B to Block A right sides together, along the center edges. Sew and press the seams open. Repeat to make three sets (quilt rows 2, 4, and 6).

4 Lay out the rows again to keep things in order. Aligning the seams, pin or glue baste two quilt rows together and sew. Press the seams open. Repeat for the other four rows to complete the quilt top.

FINISH THE QUILT

1 Cut the backing fabric in half and remove the selvedges. Sew the pieces together along the longest side using a ½" (1.3 cm) seam allowance. Press the seam open.

2 Use your favorite method to layer and baste your quilt top, batting, and backing. Quilt as desired. I chose a simple quilt pattern by quilting ¼" (6 mm) away from either side of the seam line.

3 Sew together the binding strips end to end diagonally, and use your preferred method to bind the quilt.

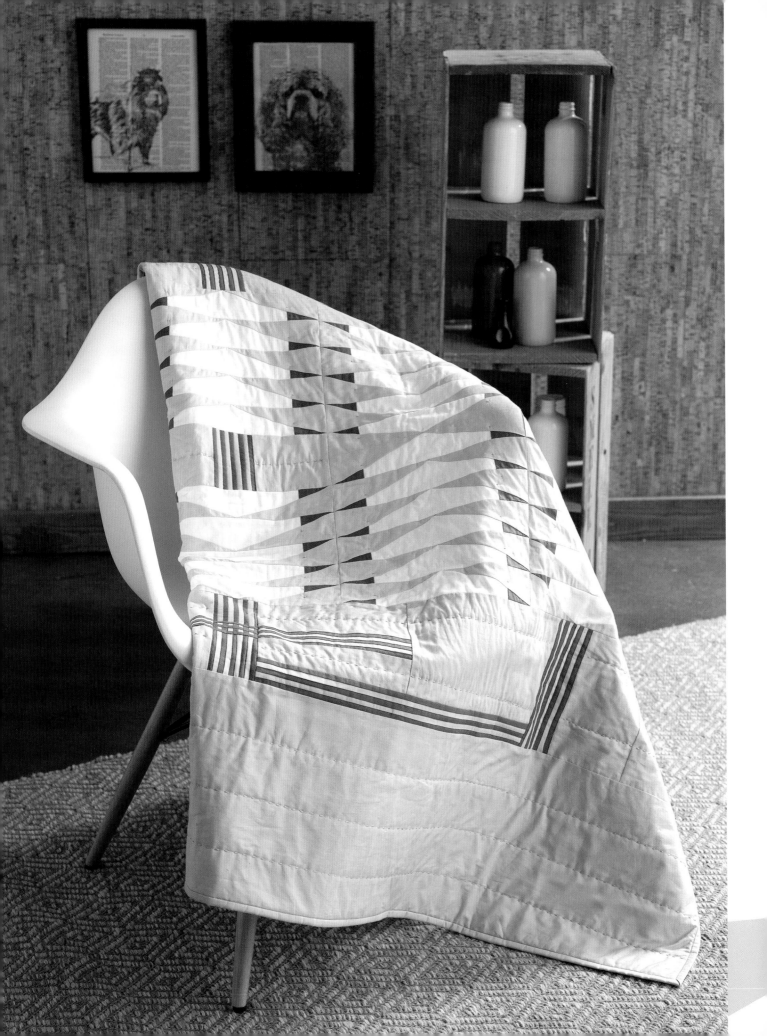

CONCORDIA
quilt

A skein of geese flies overhead against a cloudy sky and creates a bold design when the birds' wing tips touch. The dark tips and the crisscross of lines make a strong visual statement. This quilt would work beautifully hanging on any wall or used as a decorative throw. Concordia is an intermediate paper-pieced pattern ideal for anyone who enjoys small piecing. Because the narrow dark gray and light gray strips in this quilt require precision, they are paper-pieced rather than strip-pieced.

Finished Size:
45 ½" × 55" (115 × 139.5 cm)

Materials
Yardage is based on fabric with a usable width of 42" (106.5 cm).

½ yd (45.5 cm) white fabric

3 yd (2.75 m) light gray fabric

¾ yd (68.5 cm) dark gray fabric

2½ yd (2.3 m) backing fabric

53" × 63" (134.5 × 160 cm) piece of batting

½ yd (45.5 cm) binding fabric

Tools

Paper for paper piecing

Concordia Geese Template Pattern (page 154)

Concordia Block Template Patterns B, D, E, H1/H2, G, I, K, and N (pages 154–156)

Cutting

WOF= width of fabric

Refer to the **Concordia Assembly Diagram** (page 126) before cutting.

From white fabric, cut:
7 strips 2½" (6.5 cm) × WOF; subcut into 32 pieces 2½" × 8" (6.5 × 20.5 cm) (Geese Template, Piece S).

From light gray fabric, cut in the following order (keep all leftover cuttings for pieces A, C, F, J, L, M, O, and P):
3 pieces 10¾" (27.5 cm) × WOF; from 1 piece subcut 2 pieces 5" × 10¾" (2.5 × 27.5 cm)

2 pieces 7½" (19 cm) × WOF; trim each to 35½" (90 cm) (Y)

1 strip 2" (5 cm) × WOF; subcut into 8 strips 8" × 1" (20.5 × 2.5 cm) (B), and 16 squares 1" × 1" (2.5 cm × 2.5 cm) (H1/H2) *

1 strip 2" (5 cm) × WOF; subcut into 4 strips 1" × 20" (2.5 × 51 cm) (D)

1 strip 1" (2.5 cm) × WOF; subcut into 4 strips 1" × 8½" (2.5 × 21.5 cm) (E) and 2 strips 1" × 4" (2.5 cm × 10 cm) (G)*

1 strip 1" (2.5 cm) × WOF; subcut into 8 strips 1" × 4½" (2.5 × 11.5 cm) (I) and 1 strip 1" × 4" (2.5 × 10 cm) (G)

1 strip 1" (2.5 cm) × WOF; subcut into 4 strips 1" × 5" (2.5 × 12.5 cm) (K) and 5 strips 1" × 4" (2.5 × 10 cm) (G)*

1 strip 1" (2.5 cm) × WOF; subcut into 8 strips 1" × 4½" (2.5 × 11.5 cm) (N)

6 strips 4" (10 cm) × WOF; subcut into 32 pieces 4" × 7½" (10 × 19 cm) (Geese - Q). Cut these in half on the diagonal (see *Fig. 1* below).

From the remaining light gray fabric cut:
2 strips 7½" × 4⅝" (19 × 11.75 cm) (A)

2 strips 11¾" × 6¼" (30 × 16 cm) (C)

2 strips 8" × 3⅜" (20.5 × 8.6 cm) (F)

4 strips 4⅝" × 3⅜" (11.75 × 8.6 cm) (J & L)

4 strips 4⅝" × 4" (11.75 × 10 cm) (M & O)

2 strips 8" × 2⅛" (20.5 × 5.4 cm) (P).

From dark gray fabric, cut:
1 strip 2" (5 cm) × WOF; subcut into 10 strips 1" × 8" (5 × 20.5 cm) (B)**

1 strip 3" (7.5 cm) × WOF; subcut into 6 strips 1" × 20" (5 × 51 cm) (D)

1 strip 2" (5 cm) × WOF; subcut into 6 strips 1" × 8½" (5 × 21.5 cm) (E)*

1 strip 4½" (11.5 cm) × WOF; subcut into 20 strips 1" × 4½ " (2.5 × 11.5 cm) (10 G and 10 N)

1 strip 1" (2.5 cm) × WOF; subcut into 6 strips 1" × 3" (5 × 7.5 cm) strips and 20 strips 1 × 1" (2.5 × 2.5 cm) (H1/H2)

1 strip 1" (2.5 cm) × WOF; subcut into 10 strips 1" × 4" (2.5 × 10 cm) (I)

1 strip 1" (2.5 cm) × WOF; subcut into 6 strips 1" × 5" strips (2.5 × 12.5 cm) (K)*

1 strip 9" (23 cm) × WOF; subcut into 64 strips 1½" × 3" (3.8 × 7.5 cm) (Geese - R).

From binding fabric, cut:
6 strips 2½" × WOF (6.5 cm × WOF).

*Use leftover fabric for any remaining blocks.

**When cutting strips as narrow as 1" (2.5 cm), make your first cut wider and then cut down the width strips to help ensure greater accuracy.

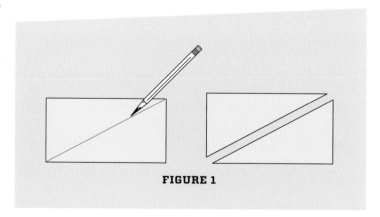

FIGURE 1

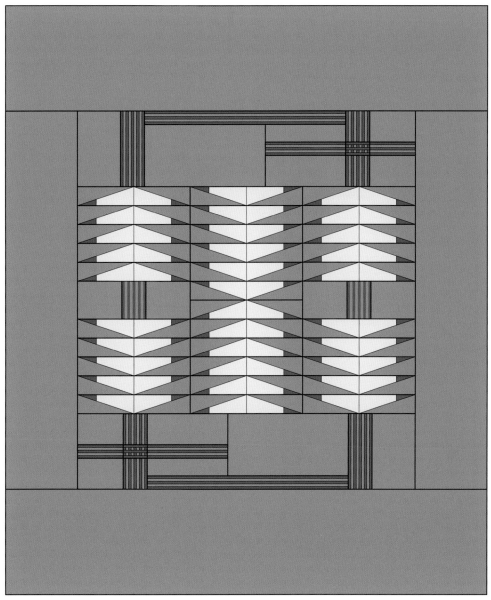

CONCORDIA QUILT

MAKE THE BLOCKS

1 Refer to **My Method: Paper Piecing** (page 67) to make and cut out sixteen copies of each side of the Concordia Geese template two copies of each Concordia Block template B, D, E, H/HI, G, I, K, and N. Tape together the geese templates to make thirty-two units (**Fig. 2,** page 124).

2 Follow the general instructions in **My Method: Paper Piecing** (page 67) to make the thirty-two geese units,

using the white pieces 2½" × 8" (6.5 × 20.5 cm) (S), the light gray pieces 4" × 7½" (10 × 19 cm) (Q) that you have cut in half on the diagonal, and the dark gray pieces 1½" × 3" (3.8 × 7.5 cm) (R). Paper-piece blocks B, D, E, H1, H2, I, K, and N, using the pieces indicated in the Cutting list (page 122). On each template, begin with Piece 1 and sew the pieces in numerical order.

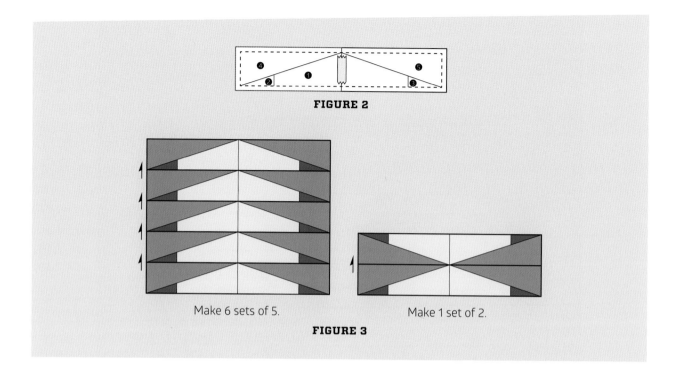

FIGURE 2

Make 6 sets of 5.

Make 1 set of 2.

FIGURE 3

3 Sew together six sets of five geese each, all oriented in the same direction, as shown (**Fig. 3**). Sew the last two geese together with the tips facing each other (**Fig. 3**). Press all the seams open.

4 Sew together pieces H1 to H2 to make two units. Press the seams to the side.

ASSEMBLE THE QUILT TOP

1 Refer to the **Concordia Assembly Diagram** to put together the quilt top. Begin with the top row of the center section. Working from left to right, sew the blocks together in the following order: Sew A to B; P to E and then to F; C to PEF; D to CPEF; G, H, and I; DCPEF to GHI; J, K, and L; and GHI to JKL. Press all seams to the side. This completes the top row.

2 For the second row, sew together three sets of geese, orienting the middle set the opposite way, as shown. Press the seams open.

Spotlight

At 20" (51 cm), the strips for Block D are long for paper piecing. To help line up the fabric, pinning or glue basting is necessary. If the cut fabric edges are straight, use the edge of the previous fabric as a seam guide. This will make lining up long strips of fabric easier.

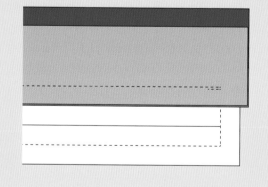

3 For the third row, sew together blocks M and N; and sew O to MN. Repeat for the second OMN group. Sew the OMN blocks to either side of the two-unit geese section as shown in the Concordia Assembly Diagram.

4 For the fourth row, sew together the three remaining sets of geese, orienting the middle set the opposite way, as shown. Press the seams open.

5 Working with the bottom row and from left to right, sew the blocks together in the following order: Sew L, K, and J; I, H, and G: LKJ to IHG; F, E, and P; FEP to C; FEPC to D; A and B; and FEPCD to AB. Press all seams to the side. This completes the bottom row.

6 Sew a Piece Y to either side of the quilt center.

7 Piece together your short piece of light gray with your WOF piece to complete Piece X. Sew one of each to the top and bottom of the quilt. Trim to size once you have attached it to the quilt.

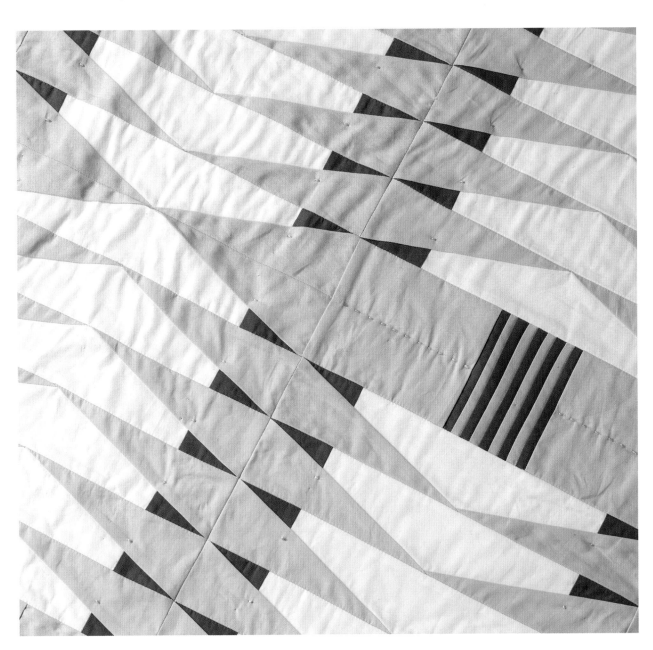

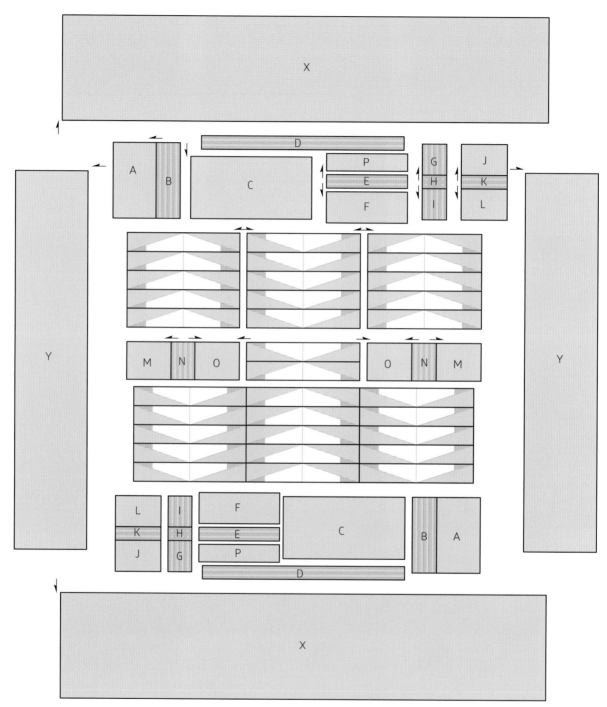

CONCORDIA ASSEMBLY DIAGRAM

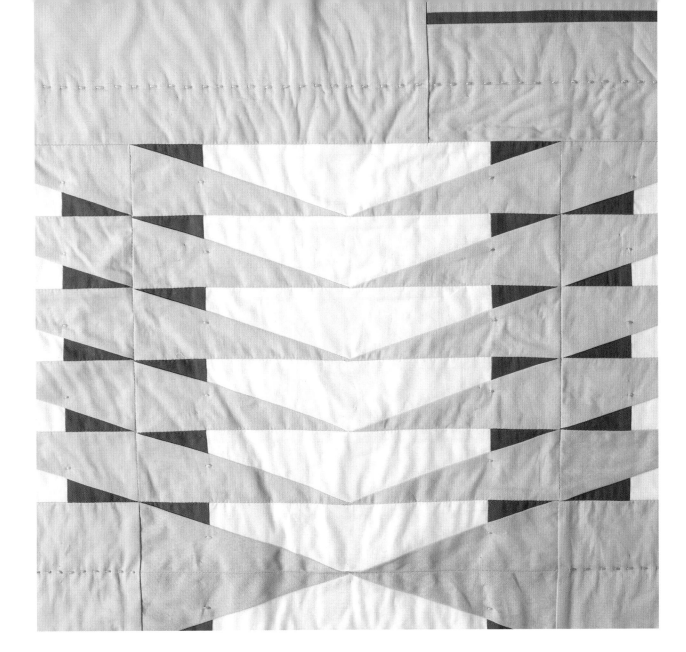

FINISH THE QUILT

1 Cut one piece 42" × 63" (106.5 × 160 cm) piece from the backing. Cut two strips 12" × 32" (30.5 × 81.5 cm). Sew the two strips together using a ½" (1.3 cm) seam. Press the seam open. Join the two backing pieces together along the 63" (160 cm) side using a ½" (1.3 cm) seam, and again press the seam open.

2 Use your favorite method to layer and baste your quilt top, batting, and backing. Quilt as desired. I chose to hand-quilt in a coordinating thread color that would not distract from the Flying Geese. It adds just enough texture to the quilt while letting the design shine.

3 Sew together the binding strips end to end diagonally, and use your preferred method to bind the quilt.

VERTEBRAE
quilt

Vertebrae is a very graphic print, perfect for anyone who wants to make a statement. Inspiration certainly can be found everywhere—here, in the form of textiles and science. My design for this quilt was drawn from a dramatic fabric from Warwick Fabrics (see page 12). To me, the pattern, with its projected finger-like shapes, is reminiscent of thoracic vertebrae. Depending on the colors you choose for this quilt, the design can have any number of looks. Small changes can a make big impact!

Finished Size:

68" × 73" (173 × 185.5 cm)

Materials

Yardage is based on fabric with a usable width of 42" (106.5 cm).

1⅛ yd (103 cm) white fabric

¾ yd (68.5 cm) green fabric

1⅛ yd (103 cm) light blue fabric

1⅛ yd (103 cm) orange fabric

1 yd (91.5 cm) mustard fabric

1 yd (91.5 cm) dark gray fabric

5 yd (4.6 m) backing fabric

80" × 85" (203 × 216 cm) piece of batting

½ yd (45.5 cm) binding fabric

VERTEBRAE QUILT

Cutting

WOF= width of fabric

From green fabric, cut:
12 strips 2¼" × WOF (5.5 cm × WOF); subcut into 31 strips 2¼" × 12¾" (5.5 × 32 cm) and 28 squares 2¼" × 2¼" (5.5 × 5.5 cm).

From mustard fabric, cut:
15 strips 2¼" × WOF (5.5 cm × WOF); subcut into 39 strips 2¼" × 12¾" (5.5 × 32 cm) and 35 squares 2¼" × 2¼" (5.5 × 5.5 cm).

From orange fabric, cut:
17 strips 2¼" × WOF (5.5 cm × WOF); subcut into 44 strips 2¼" × 12¾" (5.5 × 32 cm) and 37 squares 2¼" × 2¼" (5.5 × 5.5 cm).

From gray fabric, cut:
13 strips 2¼" × WOF (5.5 cm × WOF); subcut into 33 strips 2¼" × 12¾" (5.5 × 32 cm) and 34 squares 2¼" × 2¼" (5.5 × 5.5 cm).

From blue fabric, cut:
17 strips 2¼" × WOF (5.5 cm × WOF); subcut into 44 strips 2¼" × 12¾" (5.5 × 32 cm) and 38 squares 2¼" × 2¼" (5.5 × 5.5 cm)

8 strips 2½" × WOF (6.5 cm × WOF) for binding.

From white fabric, cut:
17 strips 2¼" × WOF (5.5 cm × WOF); subcut into 43 strips 2¼" × 12¾" (5.5 × 32 cm) and 38 squares 2¼" × 2¼" (5.5 × 5.5 cm).

From binding fabric, cut:
7 strips 2½" × WOF (6.5 cm × WOF).

MAKE THE BLOCKS

This quilt has thirty blocks total. The blocks are in four configurations—A, B, C, and D blocks—each made up of two colors. Following are assembly directions and color combinations for the blocks.

Block A

Make twelve Block A's in the following color combinations.

→ A1: Green/mustard
→ A2: Orange/blue
→ A3: White/gray
→ A4: Mustard/blue
→ A5: Mustard/blue
→ A6: Gray/orange
→ A7: Green/white
→ A8: Blue/mustard
→ A9: Blue/green
→ A10: White/gray
→ A11: Orange/mustard
→ A12: Blue/green

1 Place a strip 2¼" × 12¾" (5.5 × 32 cm) of the first color right side up, and place a square 2¼" × 2¼" (5.5 × 5.5 cm) of the second color right side down, on the left side as shown (***Fig. 1***). Mark a diagonal line from upper right to lower left. Sew on the line. Trim to a ¼" (6 mm) seam, and press open. Repeat with three more sets to make a total of four units.

2 Place a strip 2¼" × 12¾" (5.5 × 32 cm) of the second color right side up, and place a square 2¼" × 2¼" (5.5 × 5.5 cm) of the first color right side down, on the right side (***Fig. 2***). Mark a diagonal line from upper left to lower right corner. Sew on the line. Trim to a ¼" (6 mm) seam and press open. Repeat with two more sets to make a total of three units.

3 Sew together the seven units, starting with the first color on top and alternating with the second color (***Fig. 3***). Press the seams open. Place one first-color strip 2¼" × 12¾" (5.5 × 32 cm) right side down to the right side of the block and sew. Press the seam open.

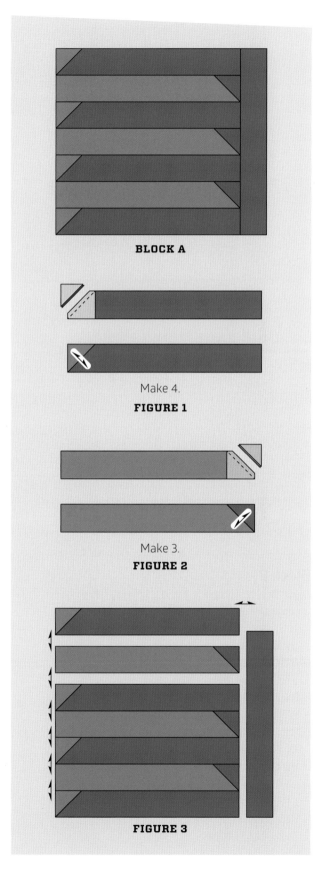

BLOCK A

Make 4.

FIGURE 1

Make 3.

FIGURE 2

FIGURE 3

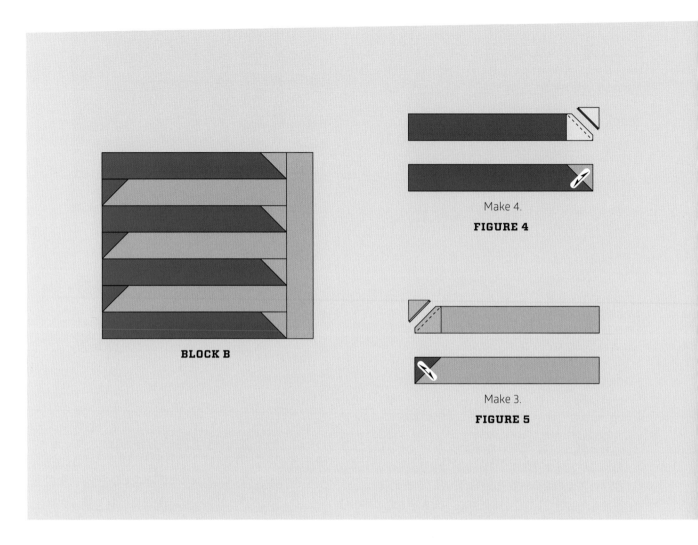

BLOCK B

Make 4.

FIGURE 4

Make 3.

FIGURE 5

Block B

Make twelve Block B's in the following color combinations.

→ B1: Green/blue
→ B2: Orange/gray
→ B3: Orange/gray
→ B4: White/blue
→ B5: Mustard/orange
→ B6: Gray/white
→ B7: Orange/white
→ B8: Green/mustard
→ B9: Blue/gray
→ B10: White/orange
→ B11: White/mustard
→ B12: Orange/green

1 Place a strip 2¼" × 12¾" (5.5 × 32 cm) of the first color right side up, and place a square 2¼" × 2¼" (5.5 × 5.5 cm) of the second color right side down, on the right-hand side (*Fig. 4*). Mark a diagonal line from the upper left to bottom right. Sew on the line. Trim to a ¼" (6 mm) seam and press open. Repeat with three more sets to make a total of four units.

2 Place a strip 2¼" × 12¾" (5.5 × 32 cm) of the second color right side up, and place a square 2¼" × 2¼" (5.5 × 5.5 cm) of the first color square right side down, on the left side. Mark a diagonal line from upper right to lower left, and sew (*Fig. 5*). Trim to a ¼" (6 mm) seam, and press open. Repeat with two more sets to make a total of three units.

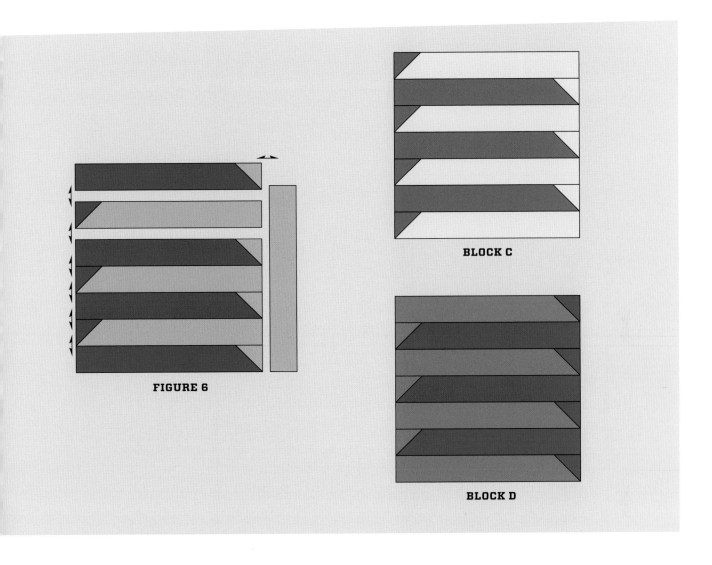

FIGURE 6

BLOCK C

BLOCK D

3 Sew together the seven units, starting with the first color on top and alternating with the second color (*Fig. 6*). Press the seams open. Place one second color strip 2¼" × 12¾" (5.5 × 32 cm) right side down to the right side of the block and sew. Press the seam open.

Block C

Make three Block C's in the following color combinations.

→ C1: White/gray
→ C2: Orange/white
→ C3: Mustard/orange

To make Block C, follow steps 1 to 3 for Block A, but do not add the strip to the right side.

Block D

Make 3 Block D's in the following color combinations:

→ D1: Mustard/green
→ D2: Blue/gray
→ D3: Blue/white

To make Block D, follow steps 1 to 3 for Block B, but do not add the strip to the right side.

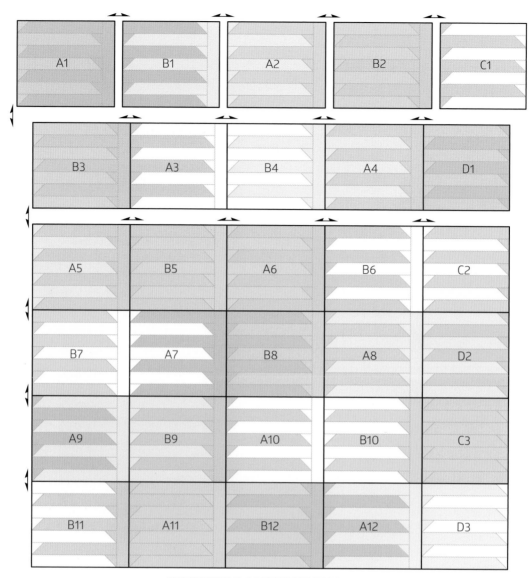

VERTEBRAE ASSEMBLY DIAGRAM

ASSEMBLE THE QUILT TOP

This quilt has six rows of five blocks each.

1 Refer to the **Vertebrae Assembly Diagram** to lay out all the A, B, C, and D blocks as shown.

2 Starting with the top row and working from left to right, sew together all the blocks in the top row. Repeat for all the rows. Press all the seams open.

3 Starting from the top, sew together the rows, carefully matching up the seams as you go. Press all the seams open.

FINISH THE QUILT

1 Cut the 5-yard (4.8 m) piece of backing in half and trim off the selvedges. Sew the pieces together along the longest side using a ½" (1.3 cm) seam and press open.

2 Use your favorite method to layer and baste your quilt top, batting, and backing. Quilt as desired. I used my seams as a guide for simple straight-line quilting across the quilt and in double vertical channels between the columns.

3 Sew together the binding strips end to end diagonally, and use your preferred method to bind the quilt.

ANTLERS
quilt

I was once given a set of antlers found in a forest in Utah, and I have them displayed in my home. Their intriguing angular shapes inspired the design for this quilt. To help create a dimensional shape to the antler motifs and to trick the eye into seeing folds in the fabric, I used the wrong side of each print fabric for the top strips of each one. So when you select fabrics for this project, choose prints that show really well on the backsides. With the yellow solid strips I also used, you can see how the "fold" looks when there is no difference in color between the right and wrong sides of the fabric.

Finished Size:

48" × 60" (122 × 152.5 cm)

Materials

Yardage is based on fabric with a usable width of 42" (106.5 cm).

⅓ yd (30.5 cm) multicolored print

⅓ yd (30.5 cm) green print

⅓ yd (30.5 cm) yellow solid

⅓ yd (30.5 cm) black-and-white print

3 yd (2.75 m) solid black background fabric

3¼ yd (3 m) backing fabric

56" × 68" (142 × 173 cm) piece of batting

½ yd (45.5 cm) binding fabric

137

Cutting

WOF= width of fabric
QSTs (quarter-square triangles)
are shown in Figs. 2 & 3 (page
140).

From multicolored print, cut:
2 strips 5" × WOF (12.5 cm × WOF);
subcut into 10 squares 5" × 5"
(12.5 × 12.5 cm), and cut remaining
strips into 3 squares 4¼" × 4¼" (11
× 11 cm) and 5 squares 3¾" × 3¾"
(9.5 × 9.5 cm) (for QSTs).

From green print, cut:
2 strips 5" × WOF (12.5 cm × WOF);
subcut into 10 squares 5" × 5" (12.5
× 12.5 cm) , and cut remaining
strips into 5 squares 4¼" × 4¼" (11
× 11 cm) and 3 squares 3¾" × 3¾"
(9.5 × 9.5 cm) (QSTs).

From yellow solid, cut:
1 strip 5" × WOF (12.5 cm × WOF);
subcut into 8 squares 5" × 5" (12.5
× 12.5 cm)

1 strip 4¼" × WOF (11 cm × WOF);
subcut into 7 squares 4¼" × 4¼"
(11 × 11 cm) and 1 square 3¾" x 3¾"
(9.5 x 9.5cm).

From black and white print, cut:
1 strip 5" × WOF (12.5 cm × WOF);
subcut into 8 squares 5" × 5" (12.5
× 12.5 cm)

1 strip 4¼" × WOF (11 cm × WOF);
subcut into 1 square 4¼" × 4¼" (11
× 11 cm), and cut remaining strip
into and 7 squares 3¾" × 3¾" (9.5 ×
9.5 cm) (for QSTs).

From background fabric, cut:
5 strips 5" × WOF (12.5 cm × WOF);
subcut into 36 squares 5" × 5" (12.5
× 12.5 cm) (HSTs)

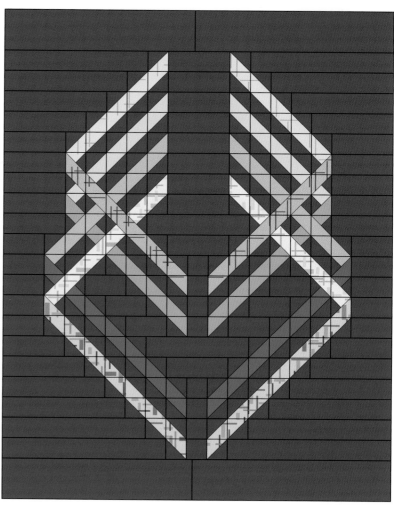

ANTLERS QUILT

1 strip 4¼" × WOF (11.5 cm × WOF);
subcut into 15 squares 4¼" × 4¼"
(11.5 × 11.5 cm) (HSTs)

4 strips 5½" × WOF (14 cm × WOF);
subcut into 2 strips 5½" × 23" (14
cm × 58.5 cm) (I), 2 strips 5½" ×
25½" (I), 16 pieces 5½" × 3" (7.5 × 14
cm)(G), and 4 squares 3" × 3" (7.5 ×
7.5 cm) (H).

1 strip 3" × WOF (7.5 cm × WOF);
subcut into 2 strips 3" × 20½" (7.5 ×
52 cm) (A)

2 strips 3" × WOF (7.5 cm × WOF);
subcut into 4 strips 3" × 18"
(7.5 × 45.5 cm) (B)

2 strips 3" × WOF (7.5 cm × WOF);
subcut into 4 strips 3" × 15½"

(7.5 × 39.5 cm) (C) and 4 squares
3" × 3" (7.5 × 7.5 cm) (H)

1 strip 3" × WOF (7.5 cm × WOF);
subcut into 4 strips 3" × 10½"
(7.5 × 26.5 cm) (E)

2 strips 3" × WOF (7.5 cm × WOF);
subcut into 6 strips 3" × 13"
(7.5 × 33 cm) (D)

2 strips 8" × WOF (20.5 cm × WOF);
subcut into 22 strips 3" × 8"
(7.5 × 20.5 cm) (F).

From binding fabric, cut:
6 strips 2½" × WOF (6.5 cm ×
WOF).

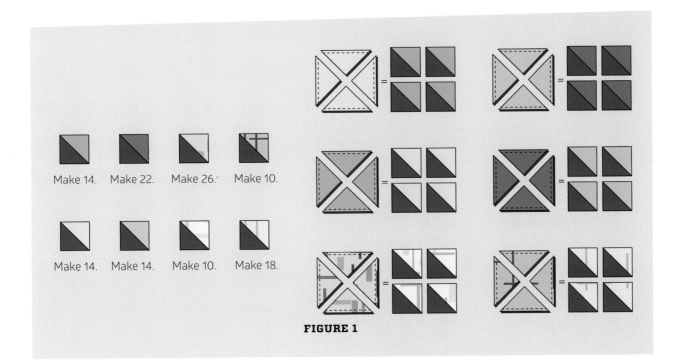

FIGURE 1

MAKE THE HALF-SQUARE TRIANGLES

Look at *Figure 1* to see all the combinations for the HSTs.

1 Refer to *My Method: Making Half-Square Triangles* (page 27), and use the Four at a time method with the squares 5" × 5" (12.5 × 12.5 cm) to make HSTs in the following combinations:

With right sides together:
→ 4 squares each background fabric/yellow solid (makes 16)
→ 6 squares each background fabric/green print (makes 24)
→ 7 squares each background fabric/multicolored print (makes 28)
→ 3 squares each background fabric/black and white print (makes 12).

With right side of background fabric and wrong side of solid/print together:
→ 4 squares each background fabric/yellow solid (makes 16)
→ 4 squares each background fabric/green print (makes 16)
→ 3 squares each background fabric/multicolored print (makes 12)
→ 5 squares each background fabric/black and white print (makes 20).

Spotlight

This quilt is made using a combination of half-square triangles (HSTs) and special X and Y units, which are made by combining HSTs and quarter-square triangles (QSTs). In order to create the "folded" effect in the antler motifs, some of the HSTs, as well as the X and Y units, will be made with the wrong side of the print fabrics showing.

Press, trim the finished HSTs to 3" × 3" (7.5 × 7.5 cm), and set aside.

Note: You will be discarding two HSTs from each set.

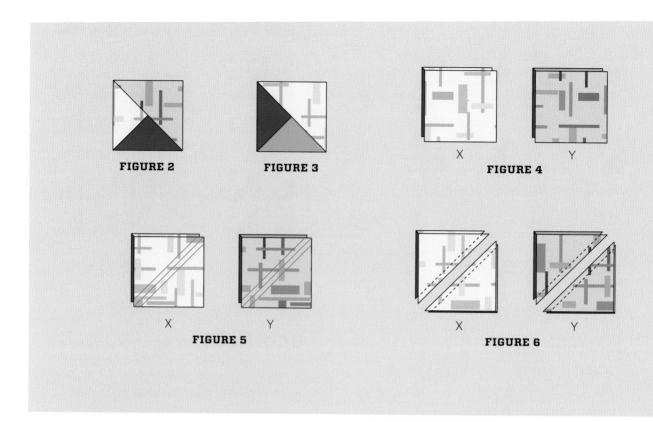

FIGURE 2   FIGURE 3   FIGURE 4

X   Y

FIGURE 5

X   Y

FIGURE 6

X   Y

2 Refer to ***My Method: Making Half-Square Triangles*** (page 27), and use the Two at a time method with the squares 4¼" × 4¼" (11.5 × 11.5 cm) to make HSTs in the following combinations (these will become your QSTs):

With right sides together:
→ 4 squares each background fabric/yellow solid
→ 2 squares each background fabric/green print

With right side of background fabric and wrong side of solid/print together:
→ 3 squares each background fabric/yellow solid
→ 3 squares each background fabric/green print
→ 3 squares each background fabric/multicolored print
→ 1 squares each background fabric/black and white print.

Note: Each right side/wrong side combination will yield 2 HSTs to be subcut into QSTs. Press seams open. Do not trim the blocks.

MAKE THE X AND Y UNITS

These units will be used in rows 7 to 14 of the quilt. Each unit combines a half-square triangle and two quarter-square triangles. You will create the quarter-square triangles using the HSTs you made in Step 2 of ***My Method: Making Half-Square Triangles*** (page 27). These HSTs will be sewn together with another square to create the X or Y unit.

The X and Y units are essentially made the same way, except that the right and wrong sides of the fabric appear in different combinations.

The X unit (***Fig. 2***) is made up of a half-square triangle with the right side of the fabric showing, and quarter-square triangles with the wrong sides of the fabric showing.

The Y unit (***Fig. 3***) is made up of a half-square triangle with the wrong side of the fabric showing, and a quarter-square triangle with the right side of the fabric showing.

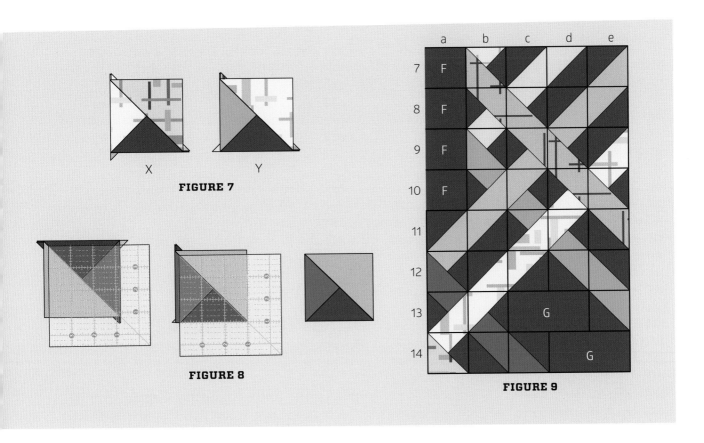

FIGURE 7

FIGURE 8

FIGURE 9

CONSTRUCTION METHOD

The following steps show you the method for making quarter-square triangle (QST) units. For the fabric combinations you will use, see *Fig. 9* (on facing page).

1 For Unit X, place one HST square featuring the wrong side right side up, and place one colored square 3¾" × 3¾" (9.5 × 9.5 cm) square right side down on top (*Fig. 4*). There may or may not be some slight overhang, but don't worry. You will trim the unit down in the end.

For Unit Y, place one HST square featuring the right side right side up, and place one colored square 3¾" × 3¾" (9.5 × 9.5 cm) square right side up on top (*Fig. 4*).

2 On opposite sides of the diagonal on the HST, mark a diagonal line from one corner to the opposite corner on the seamless 3¾" × 3¾" (9.5 × 9.5 cm) square. Mark lines ¼" from either side of the diagonal line (*Fig. 5*).

3 Sew along the two marked lines. Cut the triangles apart in between the lines you just stitched (*Fig. 6*).

4 Press the seams open or to one side. (*Fig. 7*).

5 Trim each unit to 3" × 3" (7.5 × 7.5 cm) by lining up the long diagonal line along the 45-degree line of a clear acrylic ruler (*Fig. 8*). Move the ruler until the quarter-triangle is in the corner of the 3" (7.5 cm) mark. Trim away the excess. Turn the piece and trim the other two sides.

FABRIC COMBINATIONS

You will place the X and Y units for the "overlapping" antlers in rows 7 to 14 as shown (*Fig. 9*). The following list of coordinates will tell you what combinations of HSTs and plain squares to use for each coordinate on the diagram. Because the design is symmetrical, only half of the coordinates for the antlers are provided. As you make the following X and Y combinations, using Figure 9, stack and label them according to their rows to keep things in order.

→ **b7**: One black and white 3¾" (9.5 cm) HST and one black and white 3¾" (9.5 cm) square. Make one Unit X to yield two QSTs.

→ **b8**: One yellow 3¾" (9.5 cm) HST and one black and white print 3¾" (9.5 cm) square. Make one Unit X to yield two QSTs.

→ **c8**: One yellow 3¾" (9.5 cm) HST and one black and white 3¾" (9.5 cm) square. Make one Unit X to yield two QSTs.

→ **b9**: One yellow 3¾" (9.5 cm) HST and one yellow 3¾" (9.5 cm) square. Make one Unit X to yield two QSTs.

→ **c9**: One green 3¾" (9.5 cm) HST and one black and white 3¾" (9.5 cm) square. Make one Unit X to yield two QSTs.

→ **d9**: One green 3¾" (9.5 cm) HST and one black and white 3¾" (9.5 cm) square. Make one Unit X to yield two QSTs.

→ **b10**: One yellow 3¾" (9.5 cm) HST and one green 3¾" (9.5 cm) square. Make one Unit Y to yield two QSTs.

→ **c10**: One yellow 3¾" (9.5 cm) HST and one green 3¾" (9.5 cm) square. Make one Unit Y to yield two QSTs.

→ **d10**: One multicolored 3¾" (9.5 cm) HST and one black and white 3¾" (9.5 cm) square. Make one Unit Y to yield two QSTs.

→ **e10**: One multi-colored 3¾" (9.5 cm) HST and one black and white print 3¾" (9.5 cm) square. Make one Unit Y to yield two QSTs.

→ **c11**: One yellow 3¾" (9.5 cm) HST and one multi-colored 3¾" (9.5 cm) square. Make one Unit Y to yield two QSTs.

→ **d11**: One yellow 3¾" (9.5 cm) HST and one multi-colored 3¾" (9.5 cm) square. Make one Unit Y to yield two QSTs.

→ **a12**: One green 3¾" (9.5 cm) HST and one green 3¾" (9.5 cm) square. Make one Unit X to yield two QSTs.

→ **a13**: One green 3¾" (9.5 cm) HST and one multi-colored 3¾" (9.5 cm) square. Make one Unit Y to yield two QSTs.

→ **b13**: One green 3¾" (9.5 cm) HST and one multi-colored 3¾" (9.5 cm) square. Make one Unit Y to yield two QSTs.

→ **a14**: One multi-colored 3¾" (9.5 cm)HST and one multi-colored 3¾" (9.5 cm) square. Make one Unit X to yield two QSTs.

ASSEMBLE THE QUILT TOP

1 Sew together two pieces I to make one long strip for the top of the quilt. Repeat to make 1 bottom strip.

2 Refer to the **Antlers Assembly Diagram** to lay out all the pieces of your quilt top, row by row. Pay special attention to the layout for rows 7 to 14, which contain the X and Y units. For this section, refer back to Figure 9 (page 141). Each half of the antler is a mirror image of the other side.

3 Working from left to right, sew the strips, HSTs, and X and Y units as shown into rows. Press the seams open.

4 Starting from the top and working down, sew together two rows at a time, right sides together. Continue until all the rows have been sewn together. Press the seams open.

FINISH THE QUILT

1 Cut the backing fabric in half. Sew together the two pieces along the 56" (142 cm) side using a ½" (1.3 cm) seam allowance. Press the seam open.

2 Use your favorite method to layer and baste your quilt top, batting, and backing. Quilt as desired. I quilted a clean, super-simple grid.

3 Sew together the binding strips end to end diagonally, and use your preferred method to bind the quilt.

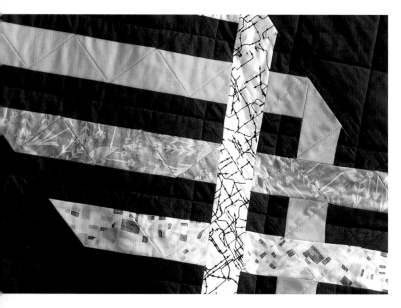

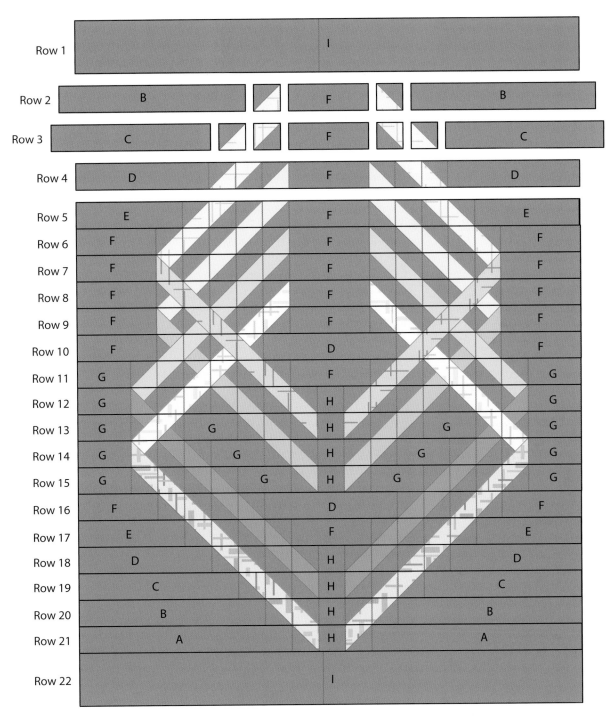

Row 1
Row 2
Row 3
Row 4
Row 5
Row 6
Row 7
Row 8
Row 9
Row 10
Row 11
Row 12
Row 13
Row 14
Row 15
Row 16
Row 17
Row 18
Row 19
Row 20
Row 21
Row 22

ANTLERS ASSEMBLY DIAGRAM

TEMPLATE PATTERNS

SPLIT DECISION

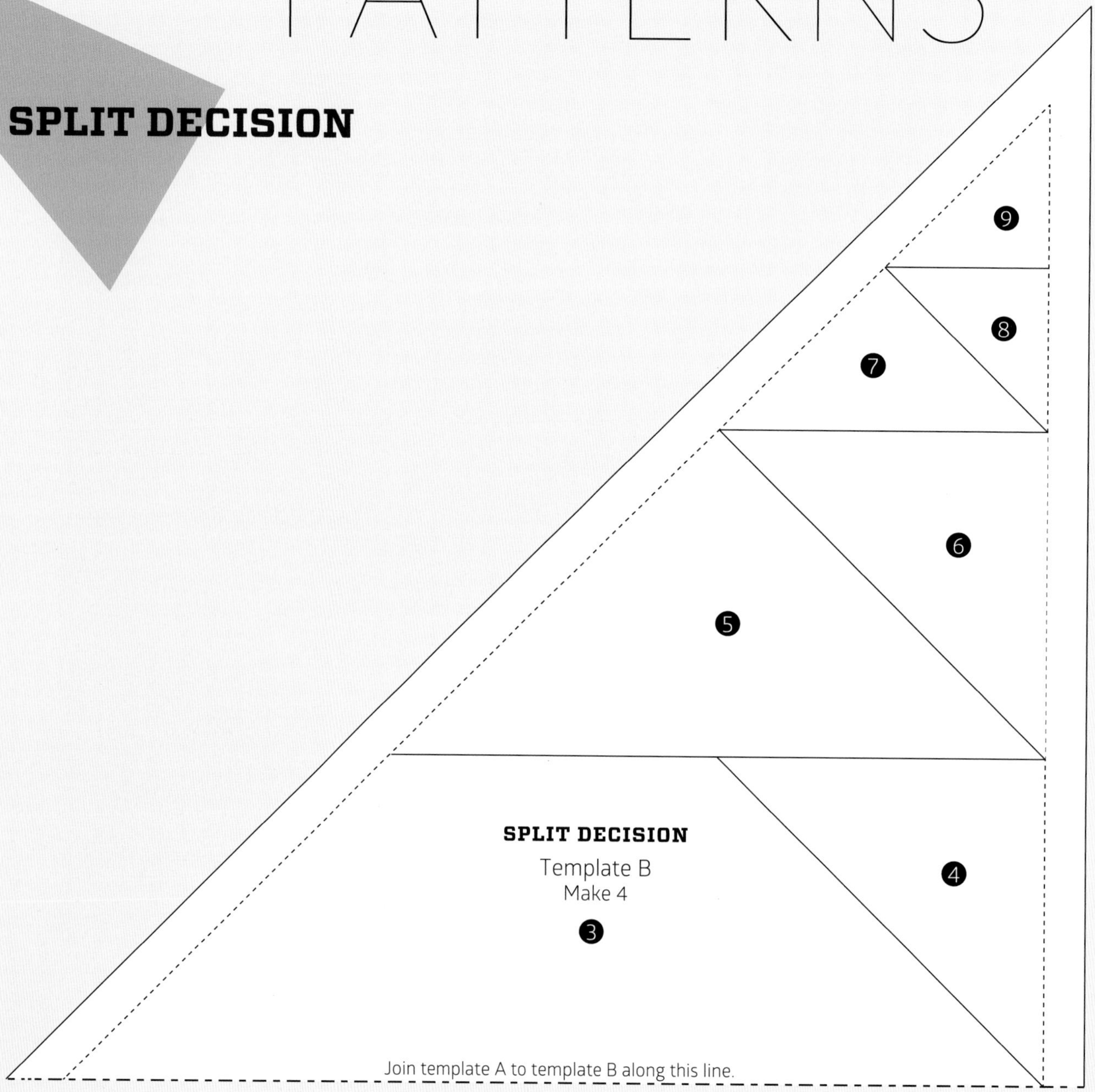

❾

❽

❼

❻

❺

SPLIT DECISION
Template B
Make 4

❹

❸

Join template A to template B along this line.

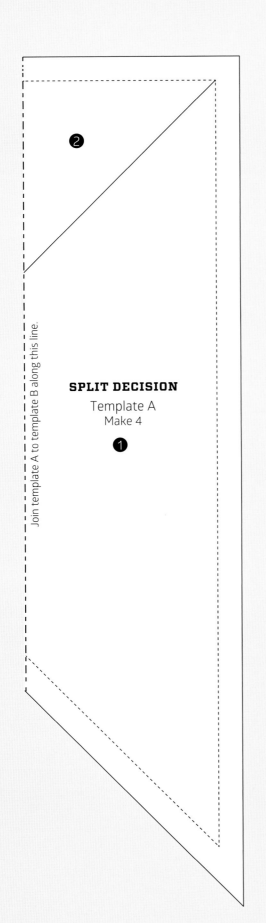

Join template A to template B along this line.

SPLIT DECISION

Template A
Make 4

❶

❷

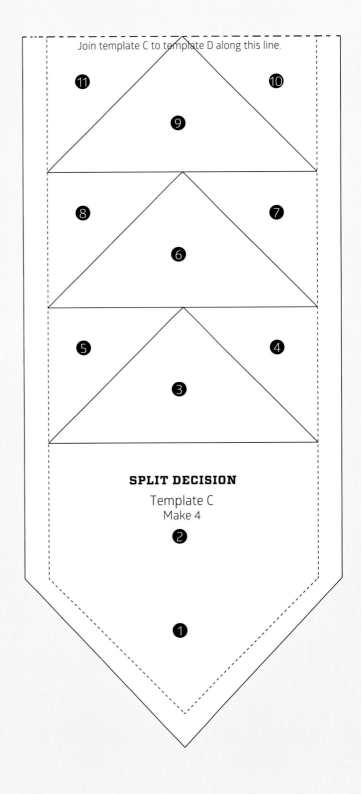

Join template C to template D along this line.

⓫   ❿

❾

❽   ❼

❻

❺   ❹

❸

SPLIT DECISION

Template C
Make 4

❷

❶

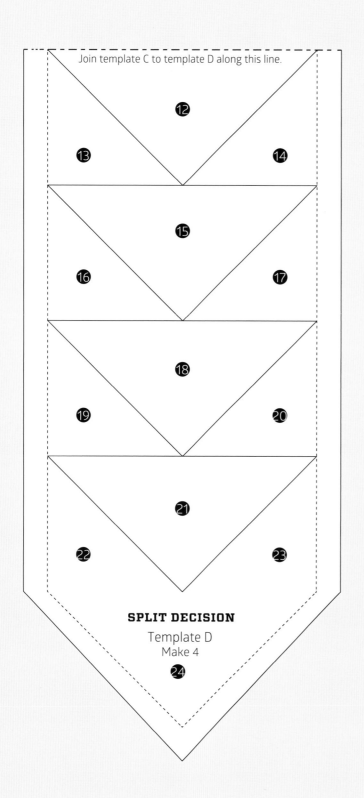

Join template C to template D along this line.

⑫

⑬   ⑭

⑮

⑯   ⑰

⑱

⑲   ⑳

㉑

㉒   ㉓

SPLIT DECISION
Template D
Make 4
㉔

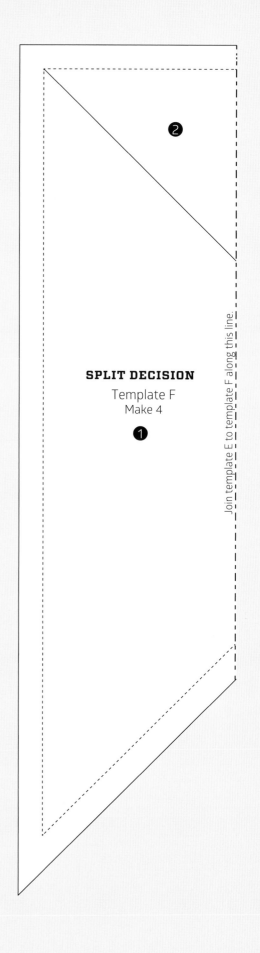

❷

SPLIT DECISION
Template F
Make 4
❶

Join template E to template F along this line.

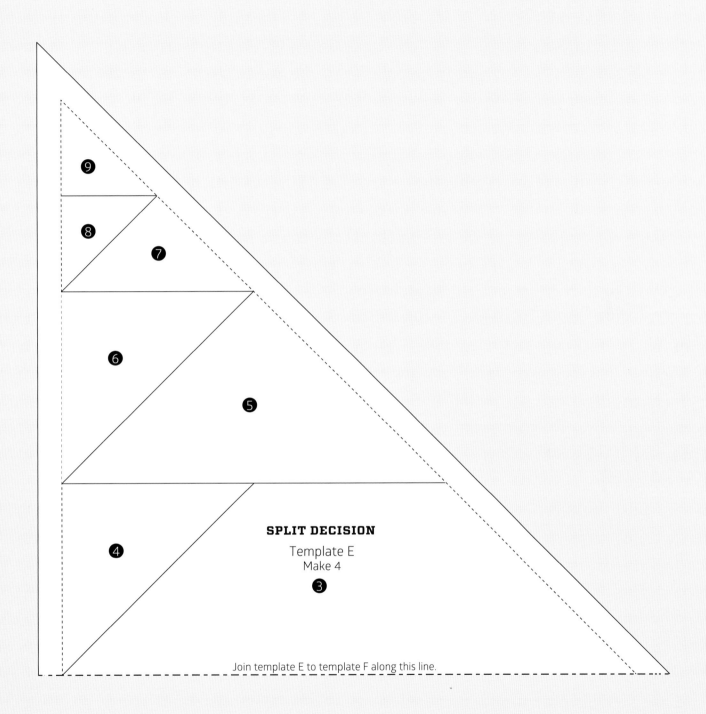

SPLIT DECISION
Template E
Make 4

❸

Join template E to template F along this line.

CITRUS

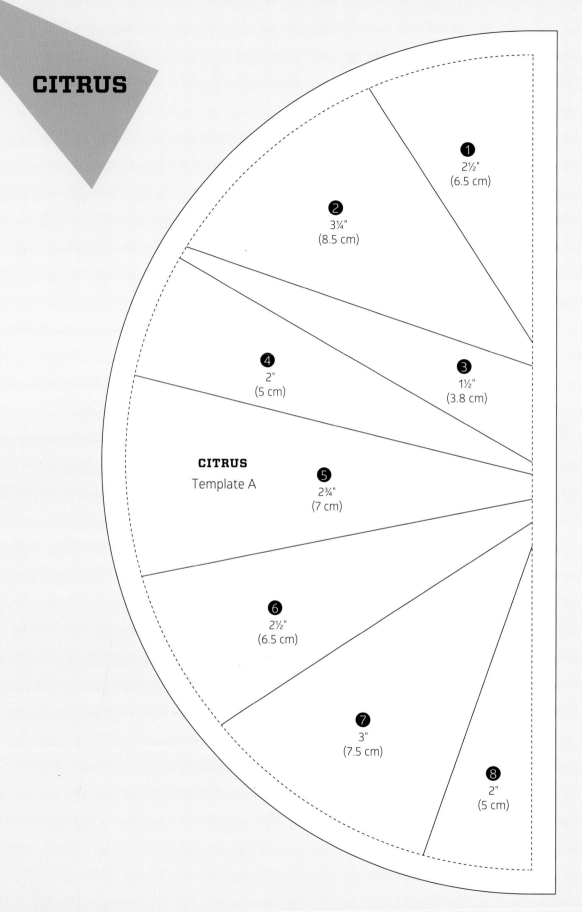

1 2½" (6.5 cm)

2 3¼" (8.5 cm)

3 1½" (3.8 cm)

4 2" (5 cm)

CITRUS
Template A

5 2¾" (7 cm)

6 2½" (6.5 cm)

7 3" (7.5 cm)

8 2" (5 cm)

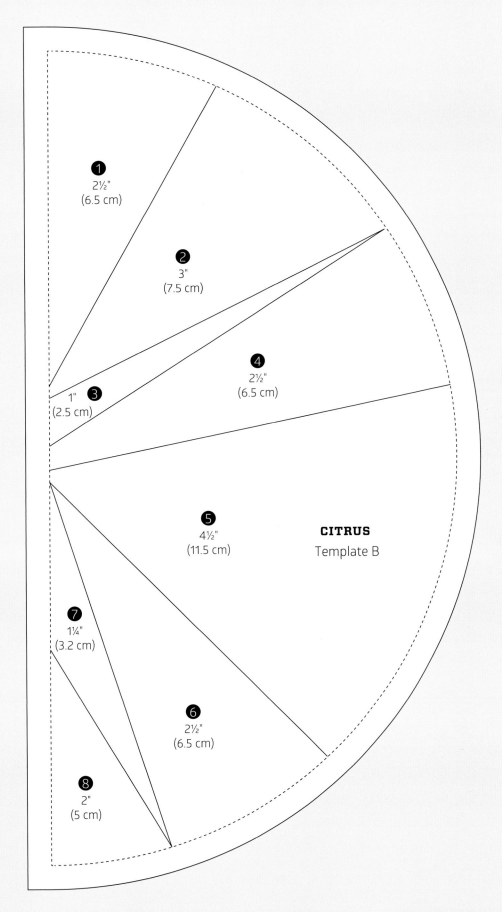

1
2½"
(6.5 cm)

2
3"
(7.5 cm)

3
1"
(2.5 cm)

4
2½"
(6.5 cm)

5
4½"
(11.5 cm)

CITRUS
Template B

7
1¼"
(3.2 cm)

6
2½"
(6.5 cm)

8
2"
(5 cm)

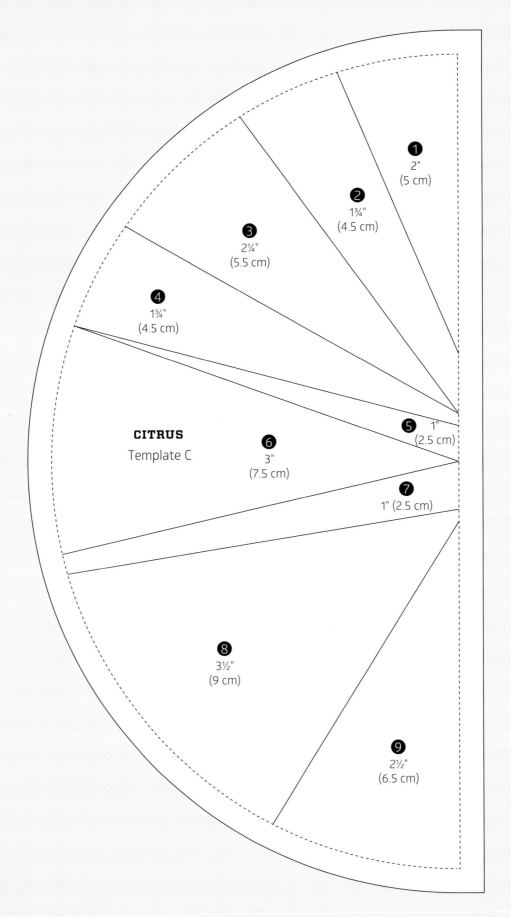

1
2"
(5 cm)

2
1¾"
(4.5 cm)

3
2¼"
(5.5 cm)

4
1¾"
(4.5 cm)

CITRUS
Template C

5
1"
(2.5 cm)

6
3"
(7.5 cm)

7
1" (2.5 cm)

8
3½"
(9 cm)

9
2½"
(6.5 cm)

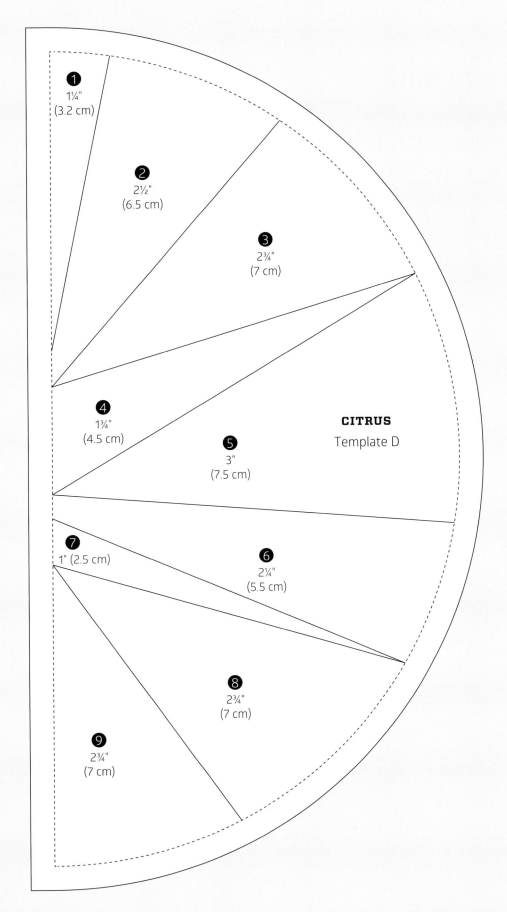

1
1¼"
(3.2 cm)

2
2½"
(6.5 cm)

3
2¾"
(7 cm)

4
1¾"
(4.5 cm)

5
3"
(7.5 cm)

CITRUS
Template D

7
1" (2.5 cm)

6
2¼"
(5.5 cm)

8
2¾"
(7 cm)

9
2¾"
(7 cm)

KALEIDOSCOPE

KALEIDOSCOPE

Hexagon
Template
Make 16

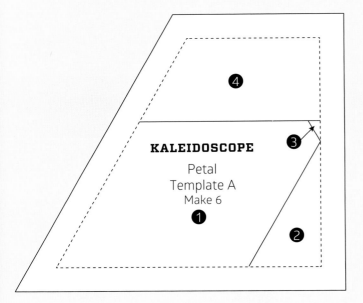

KALEIDOSCOPE

Petal
Template A
Make 6

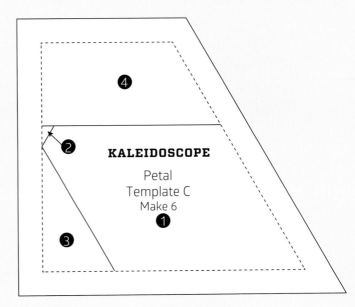

KALEIDOSCOPE

Petal
Template C
Make 6

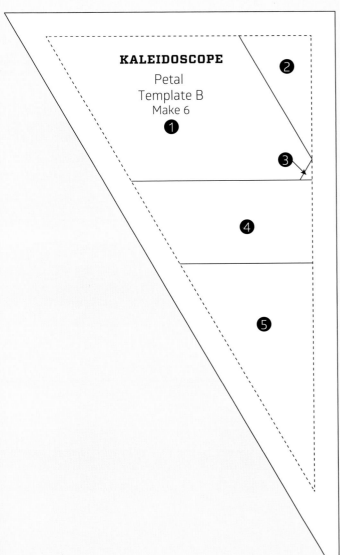

KALEIDOSCOPE

Petal
Template B
Make 6

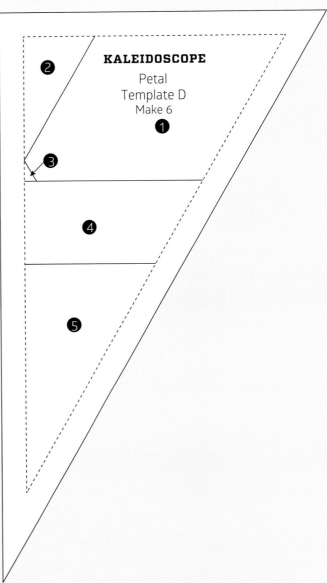

KALEIDOSCOPE

Petal
Template D
Make 6

CONCORDIA

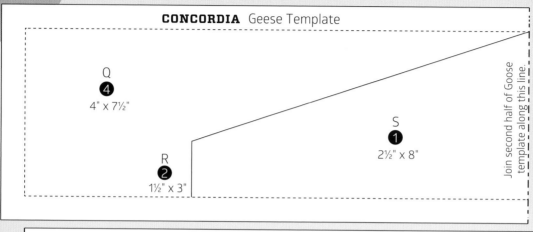

CONCORDIA Geese Template

Q
④
4" x 7½"

S
①
2½" x 8"

R
②
1½" x 3"

Join second half of Goose template along this line.

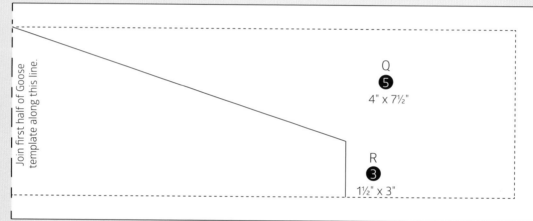

Join first half of Goose template along this line.

Q
⑤
4" x 7½"

R
③
1½" x 3"

CONCORDIA Block Template B

① 1" x 8" (2.5 cm x 20.5 cm)

② 1" x 8" (2.5 cm x 20.5 cm)

③ 1" x 8" (2.5 cm x 20.5 cm)

④ 1" x 8" (2.5 cm x 20.5 cm)

⑤ 1" x 8" (2.5 cm x 20.5 cm)

⑥ 1" x 8" (2.5 cm x 20.5 cm)

⑦ 1" x 8" (2.5 cm x 20.5 cm)

⑧ 1" x 8" (2.5 cm x 20.5 cm)

⑨ 1" x 8" (2.5 cm x 20.5 cm)

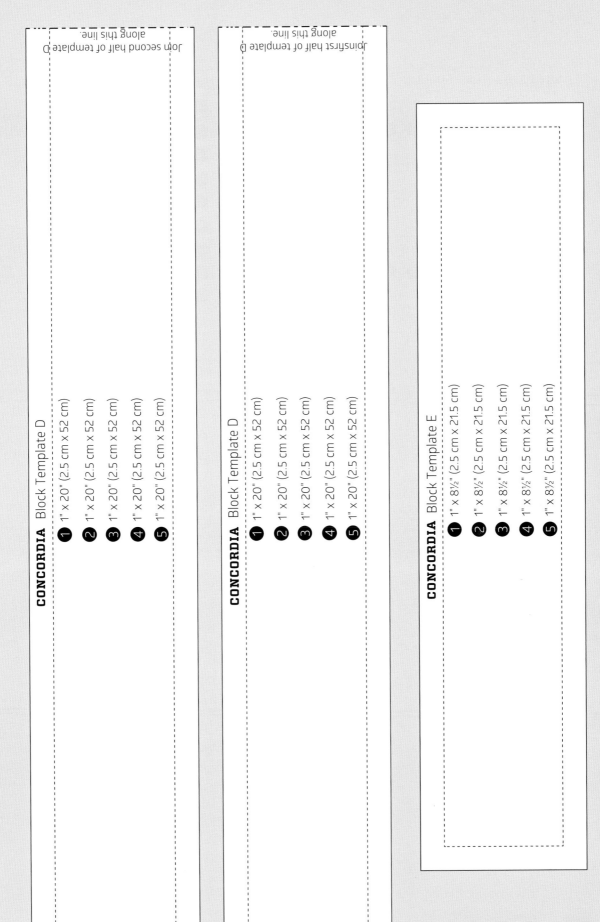

CONCORDIA Block Template D

Join second half of template D along this line.

1 1" x 20" (2.5 cm x 52 cm)
2 1" x 20" (2.5 cm x 52 cm)
3 1" x 20" (2.5 cm x 52 cm)
4 1" x 20" (2.5 cm x 52 cm)
5 1" x 20" (2.5 cm x 52 cm)

CONCORDIA Block Template D

Join first half of template D along this line.

1 1" x 20" (2.5 cm x 52 cm)
2 1" x 20" (2.5 cm x 52 cm)
3 1" x 20" (2.5 cm x 52 cm)
4 1" x 20" (2.5 cm x 52 cm)
5 1" x 20" (2.5 cm x 52 cm)

CONCORDIA Block Template E

1 1" x 8½" (2.5 cm x 21.5 cm)
2 1" x 8½" (2.5 cm x 21.5 cm)
3 1" x 8½" (2.5 cm x 21.5 cm)
4 1" x 8½" (2.5 cm x 21.5 cm)
5 1" x 8½" (2.5 cm x 21.5 cm)

CONCORDIA Block Template H1

⑩ 1" x 3" (2.5 cm x 7.5 cm)

① ② ③ ④ ⑤ ⑥ ⑦ ⑧ ⑨

①-⑨ 1" x 1" (2.5 cm x 2.5 cm)

CONCORDIA Block Template H2

⑩ 1" x 3" (2.5 cm x 7.5 cm)

① ② ③ ④ ⑤ ⑥ ⑦ ⑧ ⑨

⑪ 1" x 3" (2.5 cm x 7.5 cm)

CONCORDIA Block Template G and I

① 1" x 4$^{1/2}$" (2.5 cm x 11.5 cm)
② 1" x 4$^{1/2}$" (2.5 cm x 11.5 cm)
③ 1" x 4$^{1/2}$" (2.5 cm x 11.5 cm)
④ 1" x 4$^{1/2}$" (2.5 cm x 11.5 cm)
⑤ 1" x 4$^{1/2}$" (2.5 cm x 11.5 cm)
⑥ 1" x 4$^{1/2}$" (2.5 cm x 11.5 cm)
⑦ 1" x 4$^{1/2}$" (2.5 cm x 11.5 cm)
⑧ 1" x 4$^{1/2}$" (2.5 cm x 11.5 cm)
⑨ 1" x 4$^{1/2}$" (2.5 cm x 11.5 cm)

CONCORDIA Block Template K

① 1" x 5" (2.5 cm x 12.5 cm)
② 1" x 5" (2.5 cm x 12.5 cm)
③ 1" x 5" (2.5 cm x 12.5 cm)
④ 1" x 5" (2.5 cm x 12.5 cm)
⑤ 1" x 5" (2.5 cm x 12.5 cm)

CONCORDIA Block Template N

① 1" x 4$^{1/2}$" (2.5 cm x 11.5 cm)
② 1" x 4$^{1/2}$" (2.5 cm x 11.5 cm)
③ 1" x 4$^{1/2}$" (2.5 cm x 11.5 cm)
④ 1" x 4$^{1/2}$" (2.5 cm x 11.5 cm)
⑤ 1" x 4$^{1/2}$" (2.5 cm x 11.5 cm)
⑥ 1" x 4$^{1/2}$" (2.5 cm x 11.5 cm)
⑦ 1" x 4$^{1/2}$" (2.5 cm x 11.5 cm)
⑧ 1" x 4$^{1/2}$" (2.5 cm x 11.5 cm)
⑨ 1" x 4$^{1/2}$" (2.5 cm x 11.5 cm)

DESERT BLOOMS MEDALLION

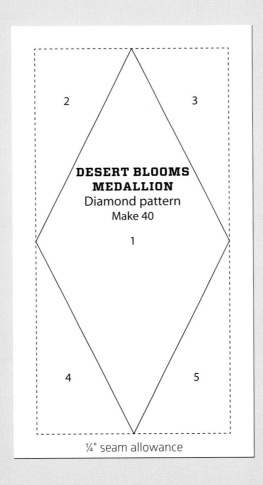

DESERT BLOOMS
MEDALLION
Diamond pattern
Make 40

1

2

3

4

5

¼" seam allowance

Photography © 2015 Joe Hancock

All rights reserved.

a content + ecommerce company

Interweave
A division of F+W Media, Inc.
4868 Innovation Drive
Fort Collins, CO 80524
interweave.com

ISBN 978-1-63250-086-1 (pbk.)
ISBN 978-1-63250-087-8 (PDF)

10 9 8 7 6 5 4 3 2 1

RESOURCES

Here are a few resources that I love, and that I used for this book.

FABRIC

Art Gallery Fabrics

www.artgalleryfabrics.com

Cotton + Steel

A division of RJR Fabrics
www.cottonandsteelfabrics.com
www.rjrfabrics.com

In the Beginning Fabrics

www.inthebeginningfabrics.com

Michael Miller Fabrics

www.michaelmillerfabrics.com

Robert Kaufman Fabrics

www.robertkaufman.com

Spoonflower

www.spoonflower.com

Moda

United Notions
www.unitednotions.com

OTHER MATERIALS AND TOOLS

Aurifil

Thread
www.aurifil.com

Clover

Hera tool and Wonder Clips
www.prym-consumer-usa.com

Fiskars

Cutting tools, mats, and rulers
www.2.fiskars.com

Gutermann

Thread
www.guetermann.com

Kwik Klip

Basting tool
www.paulajeancreations.com

ODIF USA

505 Basting Spray
www.odifusa.com

Olfa

Cutting tools, mats, and rulers
www.olfa.com

Omnigrid

Rulers
www.prym-consumer-usa.com

Pellon

Interfacing and stabilizers
www.pellonprojects.com

Pile O' Fabric Shop

Glue tips and fabric
www.pileofabric.com

Printable Paper

Graph paper
www.printablepaper.net

Quilt in a Day

6 ½" Triangle Square Up Ruler
www.quiltinaday.com

Quilter's Dream Batting

Batting
quiltersdreambatting.com

The Warm Company

Batting
warmcompany.com